YORK NOTE

D1458507

MIDDLEMARCH

GEORGE ELIOT

NOTES BY JULIAN COWLEY

 Long York Press

The right of Julian Cowley to be identified as Author
of this Work has been asserted by him in accordance
with the Copyright, Designs and Patents Act 1988

YORK PRESS
322 Old Brompton Road, London SW5 9JH

PEARSON EDUCATION LIMITED
Edinburgh Gate, Harlow,
Essex CM20 2JE, United Kingdom
Associated companies, branches and representatives throughout the world

Quotations from *Middlemarch* by George Eliot are from the Penguin Classics
edition edited by Rosemary Ashton (1994, 2003)

First published 2000
This new and fully revised edition first published 2009

10 9 8 7 6 5 4 3 2 1

ISBN 978–1–4082–1726–9

Phototypeset by Chat Noir Design, France
Printed in China

CONTENTS

PART FOUR
CRITICAL PERSPECTIVES

PART FIVE
BACKGROUND

PART ONE

INTRODUCTION

STUDYING NOVELS

Reading novels and exploring them critically can be approached in a number of ways, but when reading the text for the first time it is a good idea to consider some, or all, of the following:

- **Format and style**: how do novels differ from other genres? How are chapters or other divisions used to reveal information? Is there a **narrator**, and if so, how does he or she convey both his or her emotions and those of the characters?

- **The writer's perspective**: consider what the writer has to say, how he or she presents a particular view of people, the world, society, ideas, issues, etc. Are, or were, these views controversial?

- **Shape and structure**: explore how the **narrative** of the story develops – the moments of revelation and reflection, openings and endings, conflicts and resolutions. Is there one main plot or are there multiple plots and subplots?

- **Setting**: where and when is the novel set? How do the locations shape or reflect the lives and relationships of the characters?

- **Choice of language**: does the writer choose to write formally or informally? Does he or she use different registers for characters and narrators, and employ language features such as imagery and **dialect**?

- **Links and connections**: what other texts does this novel remind you of? Can you see connections between its narrative, characters and ideas and those of other texts you have studied? Is the novel part of a tradition or literary movement?

- **Your perspective and that of others**: what are your feelings about the novel? Can you relate to the narrators, characters, themes and ideas? What do others say about it – for example, critics, or other writers?

These York Notes offer an introduction to *Middlemarch* and cannot substitute for close reading of the text and the study of secondary sources.

 QUESTION

Are there any especially powerful descriptions of place in *Middlemarch*, and what do these add to the narrative in terms of tension or atmosphere?

READING *MIDDLEMARCH*

The writer Virginia Woolf (1882–1941) called *Middlemarch* 'one of the few English novels written for grown-up people'. Many other readers have agreed that George Eliot's greatest novel ranks with the highest achievements in all literature. It is subtitled 'A Study of Provincial Life', but that simple description is deceptive. Within its pages there is vivid depiction of life in the English Midlands in the early 1830s, but the scope of *Middlemarch* is far wider. It is a study of selfishness and self-sacrifice, a story of human aspiration and frustration, of hope and compromise.

CONTEXT

The artistically and commercially successful Brontë sisters had set a precedent by assuming names that obscured their identity as women writers. Charlotte (1816–55), Emily (1818–48), and Anne Brontë (1820–49) became, for the purposes of publication, Currer, Ellis, and Acton Bell. Those pseudonyms do not convey a clear-cut male or female identity.

George Eliot (1819–80), whose real name was Mary Ann Evans, made a major contribution to our sense that novels are not only a form of entertainment, but can also be works of art. She adopted a male pen-name because women writers in Victorian England were generally regarded as less worthy than male writers of serious consideration. The domain of female authors was conventionally thought to be romance rather than the weighty **realism** that Eliot favoured.

Middlemarch (1871–2), the seventh of her eight novels, is challenging and fulfilling in equal measure. It is a large work, but is always skilfully controlled. Composed with great care, its elaborately patterned structure enriches the experience of reading. It offers a panoramic view of a society in transition, touching on those large historical forces which produce social change.

The length of *Middlemarch* is quite typical of novels written during the mid Victorian era. It first appeared in eight half-volume instalments and was then compiled into four volumes (see **Note on the text**). Publishers at that time generally liked to issue single works of fiction in three separate volumes. The first would generate interest amongst readers, the second would draw them in further, the third would provide a resolution to the **narrative**. These 'triple-deckers', as they were known, were also popular with the owners of circulating libraries, widely used by readers at a time when books were still relatively expensive.

Although *Middlemarch* did not conform to this pattern, and although it rises far above the demands of the market place in terms of literary quality, George Eliot would have been aware of the need to raise and sustain interest through narrative tension and rhythm for the practical purposes of instalment publication as well as for artistic reasons.

Long novels allowed authors plenty of scope to portray a wide range of aspects of social life and to convey a sense of historical development. Writers such as Charles Dickens (1812–70), William Makepeace Thackeray (1811–63), and Anthony Trollope (1815–82) invested prodigious energy in their panoramic portrayal of English society and had a lasting impact upon our sense of what a novel might achieve. George Eliot consolidated that achievement and broke new ground in terms of psychological subtlety and sociological insight.

Middlemarch is one of the peaks of Victorian literature, yet it is actually set a few years before Queen Victoria ascended to the throne in 1837. This was the short reign of William IV, which saw the passing by Parliament of the Reform Act in 1832. The Act was an important occasion in British constitutional history as it addressed widespread corruption in the electoral system and paved the way for more effective and responsible democratic representation. The domestic stability of Victorian society, its increasingly prosperous and well educated middle class, with its faith in industry, progress, and steady social improvement were firmly rooted in the slightly earlier period covered by Eliot's novel.

Eliot settled in London in 1850 and entered into the life of literate metropolitan society, but she had grown up in rural Warwickshire and was able to supply local details from first hand knowledge. Embedded in her broad picture of 1830s English life are intimate love stories, developed with evident sympathy and portrayed with psychological subtlety that remains insightful and relevant. Eliot was herself romantically involved with philosopher and critic George Henry Lewes (1817–78). He was a married man and the relationship with Eliot was potentially scandalous – a more personal reason perhaps for her adoption of the mask of a masculine pen-

CONTEXT

During the closing three decades of the nineteenth century the novels of Thomas Hardy (1840–1928) presented a detailed and increasingly gloomy depiction of a society in transition. Meanwhile Henry James (1843–1916), an American writer resident in England, was developing sophisticated techniques to render the highly personal perceptions of his characters and the nuances of their behaviour. He was followed in this by technically refined novelists such as Ford Madox Ford (1873–1939) and Virginia Woolf.

CONTEXT

Emily Davies, a clergyman's daughter, was an ardent campaigner for the extension of higher education to women. In 1866 she published a book entitled *The Higher Education of Women* and in 1869 she founded the first real college for women in Hitchin, Hertfordshire. It moved to Cambridge in 1873 and evolved to become Girton College. Eliot, who had been a close friend of Davies since the 1850s, visited the Hitchin establishment and contributed to the institution's funding.

name. Victorian morality was, on the surface at least, far more restrictive and inflexible than today's morals.

Middlemarch is also a novel about the quest for knowledge and the limits of human understanding. It is about the various forms of power that individuals exercise over one another. It looks at how the past shapes the present; more specifically it looks at the choices we make in our lives and their unforeseen consequences. *Middlemarch* investigates the capacity of an individual to contribute to the improvement of the world as a place in which to live. These are themes that remain as important for us today as they were for Eliot and her contemporaries.

No work of art is literally timeless. *Middlemarch* bears the stamp of its time; we, as readers, bear the stamp of our time. Certain attitudes found in the novel – especially those concerning gender – may now appear out of date. But the distance created by passing time and changes of attitude may grant us added critical leverage when we address important issues about how to live as individuals and as members of a society. The challenge is to mesh our personal horizons with the horizons extended by *Middlemarch*. Finding common ground with such a work can be an important process of self-discovery. Perhaps that is what Virginia Woolf had in mind when she identified *Middlemarch* as a novel written for grown-up people.

George Eliot engaged with grand concerns, outlined above in abstract terms. Her authorial voice can occasionally be heard passing judgement, in a way that today we may find a little too didactic. But entering the fictional world of *Middlemarch* you encounter the beautiful and passionately idealistic Dorothea Brooke, the intense young doctor Tertius Lydgate, and the dashing dilettante Will Ladislaw. You follow the entanglement of their lives with the scholarly but unattractively dry Edward Casaubon, the graceful yet shallow Rosamond Vincy, and the hypocritical banker Nicholas Bulstrode. Many other characters are met along the way. They lodge in the mind to make *Middlemarch* a truly memorable work of literary art; a novel that can help us become more insightful and sensitive readers.

PART TWO

THE TEXT

NOTE ON THE TEXT

Middlemarch was originally planned as two separate stories, one concerning Lydgate, the other entitled 'Miss Brooke'. The first eighteen chapters fuse these two strands. *Middlemarch* appeared initially between December 1871 and December 1872 in eight half-volume instalments, issued at two-monthly intervals with the final three instalments appearing monthly. It was subsequently compiled into four volumes. A cheaper edition, the 'Guinea Edition' was published in March 1873.

These Notes use the Penguin Classics *Middlemarch*, 1994, edited by Rosemary Ashton (and reprinted in 2003). They are based on the second edition, which appeared in May 1874, the last one thoroughly corrected by George Eliot.

All the textual variants arising from the author's revisions can be found in the Clarendon Edition, edited by David Carroll (1986). *George Eliot's Middlemarch Notebooks* (University of California Press) is a transcription by John Clark Pratt and Victor E. Neufeldt of the notebooks which trace George Eliot's composition of the novel.

SYNOPSIS

It is 1829. Dorothea and Celia Brooke are sisters who live with their uncle Arthur Brooke at Tipton Grange, near the town of Middlemarch. Sir James Chettam, a baronet who owns a neighbouring estate, wishes to marry Dorothea. Dorothea, however, is an immensely serious young woman, and she chooses instead to marry Edward Casaubon, a scholarly clergyman who is about thirty years her senior.

 CHECK THE FILM

In 1994, an adaptation of the novel for BBC Television generated such interest that *Middlemarch* reached the top of the paperback bestseller list. It starred Juliet Aubrey as Dorothea and Rufus Sewell as Ladislaw.

CHECK THE NET

It is possible to find more information online about the ancient statue of the Trojan priest Laocoon and his sons, which Dorothea sees in the Vatican museum, and Raphael's devotional painting of the Madonna di Foligno (p. 213).

On a preliminary visit to her new home, Lowick Manor, Dorothea meets Casaubon's young cousin, Will Ladislaw. The acquaintance is renewed in Rome, where Mr and Mrs Casaubon are spending their honeymoon. Casaubon shows more interest in pursuit of his studies than in his new wife, and although she remains loyal to her husband Dorothea is drawn to Ladislaw. The young man has relied upon financial support from his cousin. Appalled at the incongruity of the marriage, Ladislaw determines that on his return to England he will seek to live independently. He unsettles Dorothea by casting doubt on the value of her husband's work.

Meanwhile, a young doctor called Tertius Lydgate has joined the Middlemarch community. He is struck by the beauty of Rosamond Vincy, daughter of the town's mayor. Her brother, Fred Vincy, is troubled by debt, but he anticipates an inheritance from his elderly uncle, Peter Featherstone. Fred hopes to marry Mary Garth, who is looking after the old man.

Nicholas Bulstrode, a banker, allocates Lydgate supervision of the new hospital. The doctor pleases Bulstrode by securing the hospital chaplaincy for Walter Tyke, the banker's favoured candidate. In doing so, Lydgate frustrates the aspirations of his own friend, Mr Farebrother.

Fred's inability to settle his debt places the financial burden upon Caleb Garth, Mary's father, who has acted as security for the amount owed. Trying unsuccessfully to resolve his dilemma, Fred falls ill. During the time that Lydgate is treating Fred's illness, his relationship with Rosamond develops.

On their return home, Dorothea and Casaubon learn that Celia has become engaged to Sir James Chettam. Soon afterwards, Casaubon suffers a heart attack, and as a consequence his activities are restricted. Lydgate becomes engaged to Rosamond Vincy.

As Featherstone is dying he asks Mary Garth to destroy the most recent will he has made. She refuses. After his death, his relatives are dismayed to learn that his estate has been left to a stranger, Joshua Rigg, the old man's secret son.

Casaubon is alarmed at the growing friendship between his wife and Ladislaw. Mr Brooke, who has political ambitions as a reformer, becomes proprietor of a newspaper and asks Ladislaw to edit it. Casaubon tells his cousin that if he takes the post he will no longer be welcome at Lowick Manor. Ladislaw is defiant.

Caleb Garth's straitened financial situation is alleviated when he is invited to manage estates for both Sir James Chettam and Mr Brooke. Fred Vincy passes his degree, but Garth suggests he might assist him rather than becoming a clergyman.

Casaubon asks Dorothea to continue his scholarly work in the event of his death. She initially refuses to make that commitment. On reflection she feels she must, but before she can discuss the matter further she finds her husband dead. A supplement he has added to his will stipulates that if Dorothea marries Ladislaw she will forfeit the Lowick estate. Immersing herself in practical matters, Dorothea offers support for the hospital, and on Lydgate's recommendation, appoints Farebrother to succeed Casaubon as rector of Lowick.

Brooke retires from politics after an inept attempt to campaign. He dismisses Ladislaw. Ladislaw has no knowledge of Casaubon's stipulation, but he feels it would be improper for him to be seen as a potential suitor for his late cousin's wife, and he keeps his distance.

Bulstrode, the banker, purchases Stone Court, formerly Featherstone's home, from Joshua Rigg, the old man's son. Rigg's stepfather, John Raffles, arrives and starts to extort money from the banker. It is revealed that Bulstrode's money derived from his marriage to Mrs Dunkirk, a wealthy older woman, who owned a pawnbroking business, apparently receiving stolen goods. Prior to the marriage, Bulstrode concealed the fact that Mrs Dunkirk's runaway daughter had been traced. This concealment meant that the substantial inheritance would be his.

Lydgate has incurred heavy debts, and his marriage grows increasingly strained. Rosamond suffers a miscarriage. Ladislaw visits the Lydgates, and learns of the stipulation in Casaubon's will

CONTEXT

During the Victorian era members of the property-owning middle class employed agents to manage the day-to-day affairs of their estate. This role included supervision of the behaviour and conditions of labourers on the estate. The difficulties that could arise from this mediating role are vividly shown in Chapter 56. Eliot's own father was an estate manager.

CONTEXT

A pawnbroker lends money in return for an item of value which is then either sold or held as collateral to be returned when the money is repaid within a specified time period. A vivid depiction of a pawnbroker's shop can be read in Chapter 23 of *Sketches by Boz* (1836) by Charles Dickens (Penguin Books, 1995).

designed to prevent his marriage to Dorothea. Raffles encounters Ladislaw and reveals to him that his mother was actually Mrs Dunkirk's daughter. Ladislaw realises that Bulstrode has deprived him of his rightful inheritance, and he is appalled to discover that his family history has involved dishonourable business activities. Bulstrode offers an annual allowance to Ladislaw, who rejects the offer as an insult.

Lydgate seeks financial assistance from the troubled banker. Bulstrode refuses to help him, and reveals that he is withdrawing support from the hospital. The same day, Garth visits Bulstrode to tell him that he has found Raffles by the roadside, clearly very ill, and has taken him to Stone Court. An arrangement had been made that Fred Vincy should manage that property, under Garth's supervision.

> **CONTEXT**
>
> Each chapter of *Middlemarch* opens with a quotation. Sometimes these **epigraphs** are made up by Eliot. In all cases, they indicate a major thematic concern of the chapter that follows.

Raffles has told Garth of Bulstrode's past, and as a matter of honour Garth now severs the business connection between them. Later, Mrs Bulstrode persuades Garth to restore the arrangement, which enables Fred to marry Mary, and to become a successful farmer.

Bulstrode summons Lydgate to attend to Raffles. In order to win the doctor's allegiance, he writes a cheque to clear Lydgate's considerable debts. Lydgate gives specific instructions for the care of Raffles, whom he believes should survive this bout of illness. Bulstrode deliberately fails to convey these instructions to his housekeeper, and as a consequence of the opium and brandy she administers Raffles dies.

Lydgate feels uneasy. Bulstrode is relieved that the extortion has come to an end. But Raffles had disclosed the banker's hidden past to Bambridge, the horse-dealer, and it soon becomes the focus for Middlemarch gossip. Bulstrode's reputation is destroyed, and Lydgate is implicated in the allegations.

Dorothea has faith in Lydgate and seeks to clear his name. She writes a cheque, allowing him to clear his debt to Bulstrode. Lydgate and Rosamond move to London, where he becomes a successful practitioner, and they have children. After his death, at fifty, Rosamond marries a wealthy older doctor.

Ladislaw returns to Middlemarch. He and Dorothea acknowledge their love for one another. She gives up Lowick Manor and they marry, to the dismay of her friends and relatives. The couple move to London, and have children. Ladislaw becomes a reforming politician. In time, they are welcomed back to Middlemarch, and Dorothea's son eventually inherits Tipton Grange.

DETAILED SUMMARIES

PRELUDE

- The ordinary lives of women and the exceptional life of Saint Theresa are discussed.

The novel begins with reference to Saint Theresa of Avila, whose 'passionate, ideal nature demanded an epic life' (p. 3). The **narrator** comments that many women have aspired to transcend the limitations and constraints imposed upon their lives, but few have been able to achieve that goal.

COMMENTARY

The novel is subtitled 'A Study of Provincial Life', but the 'Prelude' takes us far from provincial England, to sixteenth-century Spain and the ecstatic visions of Saint Theresa. Theresa stands as a **type** for women who have aspired to transcend the limits of their circumstances, and to make a positive contribution to the wider world. Eliot uses the word **epic** (or 'epos', p. 3) to denote a life conducted in heroic style, engaged with grand issues.

Throughout *Middlemarch*, Eliot directs our attention to both the particular and the general, to specific cases and to types of character or behaviour. That process is established here. We are now prepared to understand Dorothea Brooke in the light of Saint Theresa. Drawing an **analogy** that makes bold comparison – as here between the Saint and Dorothea – is a common technique in Eliot's work. She was a widely read and deeply informed writer, who sought to

> **CONTEXT**
>
> Saint Theresa, or (more usually), Teresa of Avila (1515–82) was a Spanish visionary, nun and religious reformer. Her youthful idealism, desire to make the world a better place, and readiness for self-sacrifice anticipate key aspects of the character of Dorothea Brooke, whom we meet in the opening chapter.

stimulate her readers to find imaginative connections that might enhance their understanding.

Saint Theresa benefited from the 'coherent social faith and order' (p. 3) of an ardently Christian society. Some of Eliot's contemporaries were haunted by the sense that such simple faith was no longer tenable. Eliot shared a view, with a number of other intellectuals, that Christianity no longer provided an overarching framework for understanding life (see **Historical background: Political and religious reform**).

Middlemarch is a novel which contains social criticism. The 'Prelude' **alludes** to a repressive uniformity in women's fashions and tastes which stifles development of individual personality.

CHAPTER 1

- The Brooke sisters and their uncle Arthur are introduced.

Dorothea and Celia Brooke, teenage sisters, have lived for a year with their uncle, Arthur Brooke, at Tipton Grange, near the town of Middlemarch. Their parents died when they were 'about twelve years old' (p. 8). They subsequently lived with an English and then a Swiss family. Dorothea is beautiful and clever, but Celia is generally recognised to have more common sense. Dorothea is a pious Christian. Her moral seriousness is evident from her concern to improve living conditions for local labourers. She is fascinated by greatness, and especially by intellectual achievement. Her intensity is seen as a potential obstacle to marriage, and Mr Brooke is blamed by acquaintances for not introducing into his household 'some middle-aged lady as a guide and companion to his nieces' (p. 10).

At Celia's request, the sisters look at jewellery left to them by their mother. Dorothea says her sister can have it all, but then decides to keep an emerald ring and matching bracelet.

COMMENTARY

Middlemarch was set forty years in the past at the time of composition. This allowed George Eliot to make even her first readers aware of processes of social change. In this chapter we are presented with a society that is clearly stratified in terms of social class. A major concern of the novel is the advancement of the middle class, the class of business and the professions, which was growing increasingly wealthy, and was securing more and more social power. The novel's title may perhaps be taken as a **punning** allusion to the march of the middle.

Clothing is a conventional means of signalling gender roles. Dorothea's lack of interest in fashion indicates that she is not content with conventional femininity. She has no wish to be merely an ornament, a pretty addition to a man's possessions. Accordingly, she dresses as simply as possible.

Dorothea is fascinated by greatness of the kind which changes the course of history or leaves an indelible mark on the world. George Eliot's novel is critical of the customary belief that such greatness is the province of men, and can be achieved by women only if they are prepared, like Saint Theresa, to become martyrs.

CHAPTER 2

- A dinner party is hosted by Mr Brooke.
- Sir James Chettam shows interest in Dorothea, but she is fascinated by the scholarly Mr Casaubon.

At a dinner party hosted by Brooke, Sir James Chettam seeks to court Dorothea, but she is fascinated by the older Mr Casaubon. Casaubon wants someone to read to him in the evenings, as his scholarly work is causing his eyesight to fade.

Dorothea feels that provision of such assistance to Casaubon would be a worthy supporting role. Chettam remarks to Celia that her

CONTEXT

The **epigraph** is taken from *Don Quixote*, a novel by Miguel de Cervantes (1547–1616), which addresses the clash between romantic imaginings and mundane reality. This quotation, concerned with distorted perception, can be read as a commentary upon Dorothea's idealised view of Casaubon.

sister is given to 'self-mortification'. Celia agrees that Dorothea 'likes giving up' (p. 18). Brooke argues that 'young ladies are too flighty' to be entrusted with weighty documents (p. 20).

After dinner, Celia remarks upon Casaubon's ugliness. Dorothea vehemently asserts that he is a distinguished man. Celia knows that Chettam is in love with her sister, but suspects that Dorothea's intellectual aspirations would make her an unsuitable match for the baronet.

COMMENTARY

Mr Brooke likes to display his learning, but it inevitably sounds rambling and confused. George Eliot contrasts his misguided displays of erudition with the taciturn presence of Casaubon, who is reputedly a formidable scholar. The characterisation of both is advanced by this contrast.

Similarly, characterisation of Dorothea is developed by placing her between two diametrically opposed suitors: Casaubon with his taste for cloistered seclusion, and Chettam with his energetic enjoyment of outdoor pursuits.

Although Brooke initially appears an amiable buffoon, his avuncular kindliness is cut through with assumptions of the inferior capabilities of women. As the consequences of such assumptions become increasingly serious for Dorothea, Brooke's foolishness will appear less harmless.

CONTEXT

The poet John Milton, mentioned in Chapter 1 and quoted at the start of Chapter 3, lost his sight and relied upon his daughter Deborah and a series of hired assistants to read to him and to write poetry from his dictation. This may be seen as an **analogy** for Casaubon's requirements.

GLOSSARY

16	Sir Humphry Davy (1778–1829), eminent scientist
17	Adam Smith (1723–90), influential economist and champion of free trade
17	Southey Robert Southey (1774–1843), poet and historian
18	the Waldenses French religious sect persecuted as heretics
19	Wilberforce William Wilberforce (1759–1833), politician and philanthropist who campaigned against slavery

20	*cochon de lait* (French) suckling pig
22	pilulous resembling a small pill
23	Mawworm sanctimonious hypocrite, protagonist of Isaac Bickerstaffe's play *The Hypocrite* (1769)

CHAPTER 3

- Dorothea talks at length with Casaubon, and envisages marriage to him.
- Chettam presents her with a lapdog, which she rejects, but he pleases her with his proposal to build cottages for local labourers.

On the following day, Casaubon discusses with Dorothea his work on comparative mythology. He speaks of his need for company. Then he returns to his home at Lowick, five miles away.

Dorothea walks in the woods with Monk, her 'Great St Bernard dog', and contemplates marriage to Casaubon, suspecting a proposal is imminent. She encounters Chettam, who is riding. He offers her a puppy, which she haughtily rejects, suggesting it might be an appropriate gift for Celia.

He offers to realise Dorothea's pet project by building cottages for poor labourers on his estate. Regarding him as potential brother-in-law, she welcomes his beneficence and shows him plans she has prepared.

Further conversations with Casaubon deepen Dorothea's admiration. She reveres his seriousness, although she is disappointed by his lack of interest in her building projects. Chettam visits more often, and while Dorothea receives him with greater warmth, she is preoccupied with improving her mind in preparation for Casaubon's company.

CONTEXT

The epigraph is taken from *Paradise Lost* (1667), John Milton's epic poem about the expulsion of Adam and Eve from the garden of Eden. Raphael is described as 'affable', indicating that although an archangel he is not aloof, and is able to communicate in a friendly way.

COMMENTARY

Middlemarch is a work of literary **realism**, but it nonetheless relies upon the author's contrivance. Realism is the product of controlled artifice, even though it may seem to offer a transparent window through which to watch the world. An example of George Eliot's craft is evident in the contrast between the lapdog which Dorothea rejects, and the Great St Bernard she willingly takes for a walk. The Maltese puppy may be seen to correspond to the view that women are mere embellishments, superficially adorning a world run by men. The Great St Bernard, on the other hand, is well known as a working dog, effective in rescue operations. Its presence reflects Dorothea's desire to be useful, even to save others through her actions.

The **narrator** refers to Dorothea's 'soul-hunger' (p. 29), which motivates her to eschew the trivial and aspire to great deeds. She believes that marriage to Casaubon will elevate her, and she sees him as St Augustine. Later in the novel he is **ironically** cast by the painter Naumann as another important saint, Thomas Aquinas. By that point it has become very clear that Casaubon does not merit such comparisons. But remember that we have been invited to see Dorothea in the light of St Theresa. Is it possible for her life to justify that comparison?

CONTEXT

St Augustine (AD354–430) (see p. 25), a very important figure in the history of Christianity, became bishop of Hippo Regius in North Africa. Unlike Casaubon he was a prolific author and wrote extensively on the issue of Free Will, our capacity to make responsible choices in a world tainted by the Fall from Eden.

 CHECK THE NET

Dorothea sees a resemblance between Casaubon and a portrait of philosopher John Locke (1632–1704). Eliot probably had in mind the portrait by Sir Godfrey Kneller (1646–1723) which can be seen at **www. victorianweb.org/ graphics/kneller1. html**

GLOSSARY

25	**Bossuet** Jacques Bènigne Bossuet (1627–1704), French bishop who advocated reconciliation of the Catholic and Protestant churches
26	**Rhamnus** coastal town near Athens with ancient ruins
26	*custos rotulorum* (Latin) keeper of the public records
27	*vide supra* (Latin) see above
27	**Chloe … Strephon** conventional names for young lovers in pastoral poetry
28	**Female Scripture Characters** book by Frances Elizabeth King, published in 1813
31	**Loudon's book** John Claudius Loudon (1783–1843) was a Scottish botanist who wrote influentially on gardens and farming
32	**Oberlin** Johann Friedrich Oberlin (1740–1826), French Protestant reformer

CHAPTER 4

- The sisters discuss Chettam's marital intentions.
- Brooke tells Dorothea that Casaubon hopes to marry her. She replies that she would accept such a proposal.

Chettam has embarked on the project of building cottages for labourers at his estate at Freshitt. The Brooke sisters have visited the site to inspect the work in progress. On the way home, they discuss the baronet's character. Celia insists that Sir James intends to marry Dorothea. Dorothea cries in response to this revelation, and grows angry at the suggestion that she has shown fondness for him.

On their return home, Brooke announces that he has been to Lowick Manor. Dorothea is excited by pamphlets, sent by Casaubon, concerning the history of the early Church. Alone with Dorothea in the library, Brooke reveals Casaubon's intention to propose marriage. Dorothea declares she will accept such an offer. Her uncle mentions that Chettam would make a good match, but she states emphatically her preference for a husband who is 'above me in judgment and in all knowledge' (p. 40). He then hands her a letter from Casaubon.

COMMENTARY

Dorothea cries for the first time in the novel. She sheds many more tears later. This is a measure of her intense, passionate nature, but it also conforms to a stereotype of sensitive female vulnerability. Even the eminently practical Mary Garth, introduced in later chapters, is prone to weeping. George Eliot is possibly presenting sensitivity as a positive aspect of female character. On the other hand, sobbing may be seen as a token of frustration, the response of someone with no power to control events.

 CHECK THE BOOK

The **narrator** refers to Murr the Cat (p. 36). The German fantasy writer E. T. A. Hoffman (1776–1822) published in 1820 a humorous feline tale later translated as *Life and Opinions of Tomcat Murr* (Penguin Books, 2006).

CONTEXT

The hanging of a sheep-stealer (p. 38) is a detail which reflects George Eliot's concern for historical accuracy. Sheep-stealing ceased to be a capital offence in 1832.

GLOSSARY

37 **nullifidian** person with no religious beliefs

39 **Romilly** Sir Samuel Romilly (1757–1818), legal reformer. He committed suicide

CHAPTER 5

- Dorothea responds to Casaubon's letter.
- The next day she tells Celia of her intention to marry him. Celia is alarmed.
- Casaubon and Dorothea discuss their future.

After dinner, Dorothea retires to her room to write a reply to Casaubon, while Celia plays the piano. Brooke is discomforted by the promptness of her response. He fears that Chettam will be hurt, and knows that he will be blamed locally for the perversity of his niece's decision.

The next day, a letter from Casaubon announces he will attend for dinner. Celia provokes Dorothea with her criticisms of Casaubon, and is horrified to learn that her sister intends to marry him.

That evening, Dorothea talks at length with her prospective husband, pledging her dedication to his great work. It is decided that the wedding should take place within six weeks.

COMMENTARY

The **narrator** presents Casaubon's letter for us to read. Its flat, dry style effectively conveys the man. It was of course written, like the rest of the novel, by George Eliot, but incorporation of such documentary evidence is a standard device in literary **realism**. It appears to authenticate the events recounted by the narrator.

It is clear that Casaubon regards marriage as an arrangement in which a wife subordinates her own interests to the needs of her husband. He affirms: 'The great charm of your sex is its capability of an ardent self-sacrificing affection, and herein we see its fitness to round and complete the existence of our own' (p. 50).

CHAPTER 6

- Mrs Cadwallader arrives at Tipton Grange.
- She is outraged to hear of the engagement, and conveys the news to Chettam, who is still more appalled.

As Casaubon leaves Tipton Grange, Mrs Cadwallader, the rector's wife, arrives. She converses briefly with Mrs Fitchett, the lodge-keeper. Then, talking with Brooke, she comments upon Casaubon's presence. It is left to Celia, who arrives at the crucial moment, to reveal that Casaubon is Dorothea's fiancé. Mrs Cadwallader is outraged. She visits Chettam in order to break the shocking news. He receives it with 'concentrated disgust' (p. 58). Nonetheless, he resolves to go to Tipton Grange, to congratulate Dorothea, and to display his interest in her sister.

COMMENTARY

The word 'disgust' (p. 48) was used in the previous chapter to convey Celia's feelings at the prospect of the marriage. It is an emotive word, but one which recurs here to convey the adverse response to this ill-judged match. The strength of the reaction amongst her friends and relatives indicates the degree to which Dorothea is idealising Casaubon. It is already difficult to avoid concluding that she is mistaken.

Mrs Cadwallader is a witty character, who introduces an element of humour into the novel. She comes from an upper class family but has married a poor clergyman. The marriage has been successful, but Mrs Cadwallader's faith in her class, and disparagement of those engaged in business and commerce, seem a little out of date in this world where money is increasingly linked to power.

CONTEXT

Mr Cadwallader is a rector; that is, a Church of England clergyman responsible for the care of a parish. Tithes were an ancient form of tax paid by independent farmers to the local rector in return for his services. They amounted to one tenth of annual produce from the land. In 1836 the Tithe Commutation Act was passed by Parliament, substituting a monetary system of payment for one which involved donation of agricultural produce.

GLOSSARY

53	**Thirty-nine Articles** the essential doctrine of the Church of England
54	**a Saturday Pie** a dish concocted from leftovers

continued

54	Sessions criminal court
54	*varium et mutabile semper* (Latin) fickle and ever changing
54	Stoddart probably Sir John Stoddart (1773–1856), conservative newspaper proprietor
58	the Moravian Brethren religious sect formed in Saxony in 1722
59	the Seven Sages ancient Greek philosophers
60	Lord Tapir … Lord Megatherium the tapir is a mammal related to the rhinoceros; the megatherium is an extinct creature, resembling a sloth
61	Sappho's apple Sappho (625–565BC), Greek poet. In one of her poems she compares a young virgin to an unplucked apple

CHAPTER 7

CONTEXT

The **epigraph** is a piece of proverbial wisdom, that translates as 'joy and a melon want their season'. It indicates that happiness, like a growing vegetable, comes to fruition only in the right conditions and at the right time.

- Casaubon spends more time with Dorothea, who expresses her desire to assist with his scholarly work.

In preparation for the forthcoming marriage, Casaubon spends considerable time at Tipton Grange, although he secretly looks forward to returning to his work, the 'Key to all Mythologies' (p. 63). Dorothea emphasises her desire to assist him.

Dorothea is keen to learn Latin and Greek: 'Those provinces of masculine knowledge seemed to her a standing-ground from which all truth could be seen more truly' (p. 64). Her blinkered view of Casaubon arises from her ignorance, and that ignorance is evidently a consequence of the limited education allowed to her as a woman. Mr Brooke, her guardian, repeats his often stated view that 'deep studies', such as classics or mathematics, are 'too taxing for a woman'. He espouses the patriarchal prejudice that 'there is a lightness about the feminine mind' (p. 65).

COMMENTARY

The **narrator** reflects patriarchal prejudice in the comment that 'she wished, poor child, to be wise herself' (p. 64), but this is an **ironic** voice. George Eliot is implicitly criticising assumptions which relegate women to a childlike dependency upon male accomplishments.

The chapter ends with the narrator's observation that 'it is a narrow mind which cannot look at a subject from various points of view' (p. 66). *Middlemarch* is both technically and thematically engaged with the need to understand people and events from 'various points of view', offering different interpretations. There is no single key to understanding, yet that is what Casaubon hopes to discover. His labours are based upon a fundamental misapprehension, an outmoded conception of the nature of the world. They will bear no fruit, and in the course of the novel they will be consigned to the past.

> **GLOSSARY**
> 65 **Gluck** Christophe Gluck (1714–87), composer
> 65 **Mozart** Wolfgang Amadeus Mozart (1756–91), composer
> 66 **Henry of Navarre** in 1593 he converted to Catholicism and became Henry IV of France

CHAPTER 8

- Chettam's adverse response to the engagement is intensified when he witnesses the couple together at Tipton Grange.

Chettam visits Tipton and witnesses Dorothea with Casaubon. He is greatly astonished at their engagement. He holds Brooke culpable for failing to steer his niece away from the match, and visits the Cadwalladers in the hope that some intervention might be made. He expresses to the rector his distaste for Casaubon.

The rector extols the scholar's positive qualities and points out that his wife's family opposed her marriage to him. Chettam remains unhappy but he continues the building project, and finds that his conversations with Dorothea are more relaxed and pleasurable than when he hoped to marry her.

 QUESTION
Social attitudes towards the family, marriage, and the capabilities of women have changed extensively since *Middlemarch* was first published. Is the notion of 'a bad match' (p. 69) still a relevant issue?

COMMENTARY

Cadwallader remarks that Casaubon is 'very good to his poor relations' (p. 69). This point later assumes greater significance with the arrival of Will Ladislaw in Chapter 9. We shall later learn that Casaubon's aunt Julia was Ladislaw's grandmother. As Cadwallader puts it: 'His mother's sister made a bad match – a Pole, I think – lost herself – at any rate was disowned by her family' (p. 69). There are numerous examples in the novel of marriages which might fall into the category of 'a bad match'.

CHAPTER 9

- The Brookes visit Casaubon's home, where Dorothea chooses which room to have as her bedroom.
- They meet Will Ladislaw.

Mr Brooke and his nieces visit Lowick Manor, which is to be Dorothea's home. Celia finds the house's melancholy air dispiriting, but Dorothea is delighted by the building's studious atmosphere. Following Celia's prompting, Dorothea takes for her bedroom the room that once belonged to Casaubon's mother.

Dorothea is introduced to Mr Tucker, the curate, who assures her that the local cottages are well maintained. They meet a young man with a sketchbook, whom Celia had earlier noticed in the garden. He is introduced as Will Ladislaw, grandson of Casaubon's aunt Julia. He displays 'a pouting air of discontent' (p. 79). Casaubon confides to Brooke that he is concerned about his young cousin's lack of direction in life, his aimless pursuit of 'culture' (p. 81).

COMMENTARY

Dorothea and Celia respond differently to Lowick Manor, and to the portrait of Casaubon's aunt. This reflects their different characters, but it also illustrates the important role played in *Middlemarch* by multiple points of view, and divergent interpretations.

The **narrator** wryly observes that 'a woman dictates before marriage in order that she may have an appetite for submission afterwards' (p. 73). But Dorothea's inclination to self-sacrifice makes her submissive even before marriage. She succumbs to Celia's persuasion in selecting her boudoir, and in doing so she commits herself to occupying a decidedly feminine space. The library, on the other hand, is emphatically her husband's domain.

GLOSSARY

74	**Renaissance-Correggiosities** in the manner of the Italian renaissance painter Antonio da Correggio (1494–1534)
77	**the good French king** Henry IV of France
81	**a Bruce or a Mungo Park** James Bruce (1730–94), and Mungo Park (1771–1806), explorers of Africa
82	**Chatterton** Thomas Chatterton (1752–70), Romantic poet
82	**Churchill** Charles Churchill (1731–64), poet

CHAPTER 10

- Will Ladislaw leaves for Europe.
- Brooke hosts a dinner party, where Rosamond Vincy and Mr Lydgate are discussed.
- Dorothea meets Lydgate. Soon afterwards she marries Casaubon and they travel to Rome.

Six days later, Casaubon mentions that his cousin, Will Ladislaw, has departed for the Continent. It has been decided that Celia will not accompany Dorothea and Casaubon on their honeymoon to Rome. The principal motive for this destination is evidently Casaubon's desire to visit the Vatican library. He regrets that Dorothea will not have Celia to occupy her while he studies.

Brooke hosts a dinner party for local dignitaries, including the mayor. The men discuss women, and Mr Chichely, 'a middle-aged bachelor' with a liking for field sports, who is also the local coroner,

CONTEXT

This **epigraph** is by Thomas Fuller (1608–61), a clergyman and historian. George Eliot's use of quotations from many works published in the past should make us all the more aware that Casaubon's own life's work remains an unpublished work-in-progress. This quotation makes an incisive comment on that situation.

CHECK THE BOOK

Thomas De Quincey (1785–1859) (p. 83) became famous for his *Confessions of an English Opium-Eater* (1822) (Penguin Books, 2003), an autobiographical account of addiction to the opiate drug laudanum.

expresses his preference for Miss Vincy, the mayor's daughter, who conforms to his taste for a 'blond, with a certain gait, and a swan neck' (p. 89). Mrs Cadwallader, Lady Chettam, and the widow of Colonel Renfrew discuss medical matters, including the health of the prospective bridegroom. They also talk of the new doctor, Mr Lydgate, who is said to be a gentleman, and 'wonderfully clever' (p. 91). Soon afterwards, Dorothea marries Casaubon, and they travel to Rome.

COMMENTARY

Point of view is an issue once again. The **narrator** argues against passing judgement on Casaubon too hastily, and suggests that we should try to perceive things from his angle.

Rosamond, who exhibits signs of femininity which meet with patriarchal approval, will later become a decorative wife for Lydgate. The doctor, on the other hand, is deemed 'wonderfully clever', as is Dorothea. Their meeting, soon before her fateful marriage, raises the possibility of an alternative marital course both might have taken. Would Lydgate and Dorothea have been a 'bad match' (pp. 46, 69)? Near the start of the chapter, the narrator seems to caution against such speculation: 'Among all forms of mistake, prophecy is the most gratuitous' (p. 84).

QUESTION

Can you feel sympathy for Casaubon? Is the narrator always to be trusted or taken at face value?

GLOSSARY

84	**an immortal physicist** Thomas Young (1773–1829), physicist and Egyptologist
86	**Tartarean shades** Tartarus was the underworld in Greek myth. Shades connotes both shadows and spirits
88	**Santa Barbara** an early Christian saint, whose father imprisoned her to preserve her beauty
92	**Broussais** François Broussais (1772–1838), French surgeon and physician

CHAPTER 11

- Rosamond and Fred Vincy are at home with their mother.
- Fred, who anticipates a legacy from his uncle Featherstone, speaks of Lydgate.

Lydgate has become fascinated by Rosamond Vincy, who is now introduced. Sitting with her mother, working at embroidery, she is clearly bored. Her brother Fred comes down late to breakfast, and speaks of Lydgate, who has been attending their ailing uncle, Mr Featherstone. Fred evidently anticipates an inheritance from the old man. Rosamond objects to her uncle's cough and 'his ugly relations' (p. 101). They discuss Mary Garth, a niece of Featherstone's first wife, who is looking after him. Mrs Vincy exhorts her son to study in order to take his degree. After making plans to ride next morning to Stone Court, Featherstone's home, Fred and Rosamond play music together.

COMMENTARY

It is clear that Lydgate is as steeped in patriarchal assumptions as Mr Brooke and Mr Chichely. He believes that a woman 'ought to produce the effect of exquisite music' (p. 94), and considers that a wife should be an adornment.

The narrator surveys changes occurring within provincial society, modifying the composition of the town and the parish, and altering the relationships between them. This small world was – like the larger world beyond it – becoming more fluid and subject to change, with the prospect of financial gain and social advancement invariably being the motor of change. The middle classes were prospering.

Within this context, significant differences between Rosamond and Fred are evident. Rosamond is obsessed with class, regarding slang as the province of the lower classes, while 'good breeding' has its own **idiom** and usages. It is his good breeding that attracts her to Lydgate. Her emphasis resembles that of her mother, whose snobbishness is evident in her view of Mary Garth and her family.

CONTEXT

The **epigraph** is taken from the play *Every Man in His Humour* (1598) by dramatist and poet Ben Jonson (1572–1637). It endorses Eliot's commitment to depicting human beings in a realistic way rather than resorting to **melodrama**.

GLOSSARY

95 **the solar guinea**
gold coin, minted until
1813

96 **Herodotus**
(c. 480–425BC), Greek
historian

103 **'Ar hyd y nos'**
(Welsh song) 'All
through the night'

CONTEXT

The **epigraph** is
from the tale told
by the Miller in
*The Canterbury
Tales* by Geoffrey
Chaucer (c.
1343–1400). A
distaff was a stick
used in spinning
and tow was
fibrous material
used to make
cloth. To have
'more tow on
one's distaff'
means to be
engaged with
more serious issues
than is apparent.

Mr Vincy is mayor, but also a manufacturer, of the kind looked down upon by Mrs Cadwallader. Fred, like his father, recognises that money is becoming more important than the old class distinctions. He points out that in financial terms Tertius Lydgate is a poor branch on the family tree.

CHAPTER 12

- Fred and Rosamond visit their uncle Peter Featherstone. He is attended by Mary Garth, whom Fred hopes to marry.
- Featherstone requires his nephew to secure a letter from Bulstrode clearing him of borrowing money on the strength of his anticipated inheritance.
- Lydgate is struck by Rosamond's appearance.

Fred and Rosamond Vincy ride to Stone Court, home of Peter Featherstone, whose death is thought to be imminent. Mrs Waule, formerly Jane Featherstone, is with her brother. She speaks of Fred's habitual gambling at billiards. Rosamond arrives, and Featherstone dismisses his sister from their company. Fred arrives, after attending to the horses, and Featherstone speaks with him alone, while Rosamond talks with Mary Garth in Mary's room.

The old man accuses Fred of borrowing money on the strength of an anticipated inheritance from him. The accusation is unjustified, although Fred has spoken of that prospect as a means to settle future debts. The allegation originated with Mr Bulstrode, and Featherstone requests that Fred obtains a letter from the banker clearing his name. Fred, aware that the pious Bulstrode dislikes him, is horrified.

Rosamond discusses Lydgate with Mary. Then, she sings for Featherstone. Lydgate arrives. The Vincys soon depart, but the doctor is struck by Rosamond's beauty, and she is attracted to him.

On the way home, Fred is troubled by his uncle's request. He decides to ask his father to speak with Bulstrode on his behalf. Rosamond tells Fred that Mary Garth has said she would not accept an offer of marriage from him.

COMMENTARY

Mrs Waule attempts to discredit Fred Vincy in order to enhance her own prospects of inheritance from her brother. Such devious selfishness appears immoral, but self-interest takes many forms in *Middlemarch*, and it is not always so easy to criticise. For example, Dorothea is drawn to Casaubon because she hopes he will open the door to knowledge for her. He marries her so she can assist with his work. Rosamond sees Lydgate as the means to elevate her own social position, and like Dorothea, she senses that she is entering 'the great epoch of her life' (p. 118). Initially Lydgate, who has seen something of the world, is resistant to Rosamond's charm. But he succumbs to her allure, and part of her attraction is that she will be a decorative adornment for an ambitious man settling into middle class communal life.

The love between Fred and Mary, on the other hand, seems to be against the self-interest of either. Fred shows no promise that he will be a reliable husband; Mary is considered plain (especially when compared to Rosamond), and is from a lower social class. Their relationship takes a long time to blossom, but it is rooted in genuine friendship. That is a recipe for success which most other couples portrayed here do not possess, although it can be seen to underpin the marriage of Mary's parents, and of the Cadwalladers.

> **? QUESTION**
>
> George Eliot is very critical of the narrow domestic role assigned to most women in Victorian England. Which other writers of her time share her view?

GLOSSARY

109	an articled pupil a pupil who takes on some teaching duties, while receiving an education
111	Josephus Flavius Josephus (AD37–100), Jewish historian
111	Culpepper Sir Thomas Culpepper, seventeenth-century writer on money lending
111	Klopstock's Messiah Friedrich Klopstock, German poet whose Messiah (1773) was a religious epic written in imitation of Milton

continued

111	**the Gentleman's magazine** conservative periodical founded in 1731
114	***il y en a pour tous les goûts*** (French) there is something for all tastes
116	**old Overreach** Sir Giles Overreach, villain in Philip Massinger's play, *A New Way to Pay Old Debts* (1633)

CHAPTER 13

- Mr Vincy visits Mr Bulstrode, seeking a letter clearing his son of financial impropriety.

CONTEXT
Fever hospitals were built to isolate from the community patients suffering from infectious diseases such as cholera and typhoid. A movement to provide such hospitals in poorly sanitised provincial towns had grown since the 1780s, but they came into existence in an unsystematic way, often depending upon private benefactors. The London Fever Hospital was not opened until 1802. A cholera epidemic reached England late in 1831.

Mr Vincy visits Bulstrode's office. He has to wait while the banker talks with Lydgate. Bulstrode has been entrusted with overseeing the development of the new fever hospital. He asks the doctor to support the candidacy of Mr Tyke, rather than Mr Farebrother, to become hospital chaplain. Lydgate admits that his interest lies with physical rather than spiritual welfare.

After Lydgate's departure, Vincy and Bulstrode discuss Fred, and Featherstone's challenge to him. Bulstrode refuses to cooperate, expressing pious disapproval of the manner of Fred's upbringing. Vincy loses his temper. Bulstrode then says he will consult his wife, Vincy's sister, and will send a letter.

COMMENTARY

Bulstrode feels an affinity with Lydgate as an outsider in Middlemarch. The banker is a powerful man, but he has not really been accepted by the community. Strong religious convictions feed his zeal in supporting the new hospital. Lydgate, on the other hand, is concerned to elevate the reputation of his profession by improving its practices. He sees the fever hospital not merely as of immediate practical use, but as the potential centre for a medical school. He shares the reforming spirit of the times, yet exhibits a dogged commitment to his own work, comparable to that shown by Casaubon.

In Chapter 15 we are told that Lydgate regards the medical profession as 'the most direct alliance between intellectual conquest and the social good' (p. 145). In his plan 'to do good small work for Middlemarch, and great work for the world' (p. 149) he combines Dorothea's compassionate local concerns and her husband's grander conception.

CHAPTER 14

- Fred Vincy takes the letter from Bulstrode to Featherstone, and is given one hundred pounds.
- Mary Garth tells him she will not marry an idle man who incurs debts.

A letter arrives carrying the requested testimony from Bulstrode. Fred takes it to Featherstone. The old man attempts to humiliate Fred, but eventually gives him one hundred pounds. This falls short of the amount required to settle his debts. Fred burns the letter, and is relieved to be able to depart when Simmons, a bailiff, arrives to discuss the old man's farm. Mary Garth tells Fred she would not marry an idle debtor. He lodges eighty pounds with his mother towards payment of the one hundred and sixty pounds he owes. Mary's father has acted as signatory towards security for the debt, so he would pay the specified amount if Fred failed to do so.

COMMENTARY

Fred laments that 'a woman is never in love with any one she has always known – ever since she can remember; as a man often is. It is always some new fellow who strikes a girl' (p. 138). We are reminded here of Lydgate's allure for Rosamond – certainly enhanced by him being a newcomer. In fact, Mary reciprocates Fred's feelings, developed over the years, and, although it is concealed for much of the novel, there is an enduring strength in their relationship.

GLOSSARY

138 Brenda Troil Brenda and Minna Troil, Mordaunt Merton, and Cleveland are characters in Walter Scott's novel *The Pirate* (1822); Waverley and Flora MacIvor are characters in Scott's *Waverley* (1814)

138 Olivia and Sophia Primrose characters in Oliver Goldsmith's *The Vicar of Wakefield* (1766)

138 Corinne eponymous heroine of a novel by Madame de Staël (1807)

CHAPTER 15

- Lydgate's character, his background, and his aspirations are discussed.

The state of medicine in 1829 is considered. Lydgate, who is a focus for imaginative speculation amongst local people, is reputedly more clever than most doctors. There is an account of his past and description of his character. He is concerned to add to medical knowledge, to advance the profession and reform its practice. The story of his youthful romance in Paris is told. He proposed marriage to an actress, but was horrified to discover that she had deliberately murdered her husband on stage, while performing a melodrama.

CHECK THE BOOK

After one of numerous digressions in his novel *Jonathan Wild* (1743) (Penguin Books, 2003), Book III, Chapter xi, Fielding concludes, 'this being a subdigression, I return to my digression'.

COMMENTARY

The complex plot of *Middlemarch* should not distract us from consideration of the **narrative voice**. Here the **narrator** muses on the tendency of novelist Henry Fielding (1707–54) to make interventions, introducing personal comments and digressions. It is suggested that Fielding lived in a more relaxed age; there is no longer time for such a leisurely approach. Fielding's voice passed authoritative moral judgements in his novels. For George Eliot the world was no longer so clear cut, and her narrative voice is altogether more complex.

Lydgate is driven by concern for his profession, but also by the spirit of adventure. Pathology is compared to the continent of America, which in 1829 still offered extensive opportunities for exploration of uncharted territory.

The melodramatic tale of Lydgate's Parisian infatuation starkly contrasts with the narrowly provincial propriety of Middlemarch. It discloses a passionate element within Lydgate's character, which seems now to have become largely subordinated to the demands of his work.

Lydgate's intellectual hero is the French physiologist Bichat, who considered bodily tissues to be 'ultimate facts in the living organism, marking the limit of anatomical analysis'. Lydgate aspires to advance beyond this position, and to discover the 'primitive tissue' from which all others are derived (p. 148). His research offers a clear parallel to that of Casaubon, who seeks the key to mythologies. One man works with myth, the other with science, but neither attains their goal. George Eliot seems to suggest that the desire to discover points of origin and keys to total knowledge was no longer tenable in the late nineteenth century (see **Historical background: Political and religious reform**).

Bichat held that living organisms had to be regarded as 'consisting of certain primary webs or tissues' (p. 148). This scientific belief offers a **metaphor** for the view of human life presented in *Middlemarch*. No character can be viewed in isolation; individuals are caught up in webs of relationships with others, and it is these relationships, rather than personal desires, that tend to determine their fate.

CONTEXT

Marie François Xavier Bichat (1771–1802) was a pioneering anatomist and physiologist. His post mortem dissection of human bodies led him to conclude that tissues are the basic units of life.

CONTEXT

'[A] recent legal decision' (p. 147) refers to a case enforcing the Apothecaries Act (1815), which insisted that dispensing chemists should be suitably qualified.

GLOSSARY

143	Rasselas *Rasselas* (1759), fictional work by Samuel Johnson (1709–84)
143	Gulliver *Gulliver's Travels* (1726), satirical work by Jonathan Swift (1667–1745)
143	Bailey's Dictionary Nathan Bailey's *A Universal Etymological Dictionary* (1721)
143	*Chrysal, or the Adventures of a Guinea* satirical work by Charles Johnstone, published 1760–5
144	'makdom and her fairnesse' form and beauty, from an essay on poetry by James I (1566–1625)
145	Jenner Edward Jenner (1749–1823), pioneer of vaccination
146	Herschel Sir William Herschel (1738–1822), astronomer
150	Saint-Simonians followers of the Utopian socialist, Comte de Saint-Simon (1760–1825)
150	Offenbach Jacques Offenbach (1819–80), composer

CHAPTER 16

- A dinner party is held at Mr Vincy's.
- The contest between Farebrother and Tyke to become chaplain to the New Hospital is discussed.
- The conversation shifts to the attractiveness of Rosamond Vincy, who entertains the company with her piano playing.
- Afterwards, Lydgate returns home to his medical studies.

Lydgate attends Mr Vincy's dinner party. Mr Chichely, the coroner, and Dr Sprague, the town's senior surgeon, are also present. Tyke's candidacy to be salaried chaplain to the hospital is discussed. Lydgate recognises the social power exercised by Bulstrode. The mayor favours the companionable Farebrother against the dry and doctrinaire Tyke. Lydgate says his choice will be made according to the prospects for Reform. Mention of Reform unsettles the older men.

Rosamond talks to Lydgate with a liveliness that makes Chichely feel jealous. Lydgate is enchanted by Rosamond's piano playing. Mr Farebrother arrives, and while he plays whist, Lydgate observes in him 'a striking mixture of the shrewd and the mild' (p. 167). Returning home, Lydgate weighs the merits of Farebrother against his own need for the influential Bulstrode's support. Rosamond is a secondary consideration to him at this point.

At home, he immerses himself in medical study. He is pleased to have chosen a profession that requires 'the highest intellectual strain' while keeping him 'in good warm contact with his neighbours' (p. 165).

COMMENTARY

In contrast to the altruism of Dorothea and Lydgate, Bulstrode indulges, like old Featherstone, in 'a sort of vampire's feast in the sense of mastery' (p. 156): despite his overt piety, the banker is perceived as a man who derives pleasure from exercising control over others.

Lydgate recognises the good humour of the Vincy household. Nonetheless, he views dinner parties as 'a wretched waste' (p. 162). Like Casaubon, he considers social life an impediment to the serious business of his work. That attitude bodes no better for his relationship with Rosamond than for Casaubon's with Dorothea.

Lydgate admires Rosamond because she is 'polished, refined, docile' (p. 164). The concluding adjective discloses his requirement of obedience from a woman. Once they are married, Lydgate will discover that Rosamond is by no means 'docile'. The **narrator** does not conceal the immense distance separating their points of view: 'Poor Lydgate! or shall I say, Poor Rosamond! Each lived in a world of which the other knew nothing' (p. 165).

CONTEXT

Women's dress was a topic of heated debate at the time *Middlemarch* was written. Soon afterwards, in 1881, the Rational Dress Society was formed in London with the aim of reforming assumptions about clothing, especially for women. It was particularly hostile to the fashion for tight and rigid corsets.

GLOSSARY

157	Wakley Thomas Wakley (1795–1862), founder in 1823 of the medical journal *The Lancet*
158	prick-eared priggish. The term derives from the close-cropped hair of Oliver Cromwell's followers
161	Haydn's canzonets songs by Josef Haydn (1732–1809)
161	*'Voi, che sapete'* ... *'Batti, batti'* quotations from Mozart's operas *The Marriage of Figaro* (1786) and *Don Giovanni* (1787)
161	Niobe in Greek myth, a boastful mother, turned to stone by Apollo and Artemis
164	Louis Pierre Louis (1781–1872), French authority on typhoid
167	'Lalla Rookh' narrative poem by Thomas Moore, published in 1817

CHAPTER 17

CHECK THE BOOK

Compare Eliot's gentle prompting of our interpretation through her choice of names for these characters with the splendid yet less subtle guidance given by her contemporary Charles Dickens (1812–70). He uses names such as Uriah Heep for an obsequious character in *David Copperfield* (1850), Gradgrind for a grimly factual and dictatorial school teacher in *Hard Times* (1854), and Podsnap for a pompous figure in *Our Mutual Friend* (1864).

• Lydgate visits Farebrother's parsonage and meets his family.

Lydgate visits Farebrother's parsonage, and meets his elder sister Winifred, their mother, and her sister, Miss Noble. After tea the two men retire to the parson's study. Farebrother refers to the divisions in Middlemarch life, and mentions Bulstrode's hostility to him. Lydgate defends the banker's good ideas, deeds, and intentions. Farebrother says he will value Lydgate's friendship even if the doctor feels compelled to vote against him.

COMMENTARY

Mrs Farebrother is disparaging of pretentious sermons when she says: 'When you get me a good man made out of arguments, I will get you a good dinner with reading you the cookery-book' (p. 170). But her point can be applied equally to the work undertaken by both Casaubon and Lydgate. In neither case does their research enable them to live more successfully with others. Lydgate is investigating the human body as a web of relationships, but he is unable to recognise the comparable web which binds individuals within the body of society. His judgement is accordingly blinkered and he sustains a naive view of his own independence.

The warm portrayal of Farebrother's family prepares us to favour him over the zealously doctrinaire Tyke. Their names illustrate well the artifice George Eliot employs to guide our reading. The sound of Farebrother suggests fairness and fraternity, while the word Tyke denotes a person with rough manners. Farebrother's considerate and tolerant character is summed up in his declaration, 'I don't translate my own convenience into other people's duties' (p. 175). He refuses to impose on other people his own point of view.

GLOSSARY

172	*Aphis brassicae* garden pest that feeds on cabbages
172	Philomicron (Greek) lover of small things
173	Pythagorean community Utopian community of the kind formed by the Greek philosopher Pythagoras in the sixth century BC
173	Robert Brown (1773–1853), botanist
174	*amour-propre* (French) vanity; the term actually means self-esteem, but it is often used to indicate an excess of that quality

CHAPTER 18

- The vote for the chaplaincy takes place. Lydgate, who has the deciding vote, supports Tyke.

Some weeks later, the election to the chaplaincy takes place. In the interim, Lydgate has come to like Farebrother more and more, and he remains uncertain how to vote.

At the hospital, Dr Sprague, the other surgeons, and some of the directors have assembled. Sprague and another local doctor named Minchin both resent Bulstrode's intervention into Middlemarch life. Wrench and Toller disparage Lydgate as Bulstrode's lackey.

Frank Hawley, lawyer and town-clerk, points out that Farebrother has been doing the work without pay, and should now be remunerated for his efforts. The vote takes place. The casting vote falls to Lydgate. He sides with Tyke, who consequently becomes Chaplain to the Infirmary. Lydgate is uneasy about his decision.

COMMENTARY

This meeting is the crucial occasion where Lydgate begins to realise that he cannot act according to 'his unmixed resolutions of independence and his select purpose'. Here he feels 'the hampering threadlike pressure of small social conditions, and their frustrating

CONTEXT

In the Anglican Church and in numerous other denominations, a chaplain is a clergyman who tends to the religious needs of people who are not members of a regular congregation or who are unable to attend church services due to reasons such as poor health, physical confinement, or professional obligation.

GLOSSARY

181 Pope's *Essay on Man* poem published in 1733 by Alexander Pope (1688–1744)

187 Prodicus author in the fifth century BC of 'The Choice of Hercules'

187 the Nessus shirt garment soaked in the poisoned blood of the centaur Nessus, which killed Hercules when he wore it

complexity' (p. 180). He is being shaped within the web of Middlemarch life.

CHAPTER 19

- In Rome, Ladislaw, with his friend Naumann, sees Dorothea in the Vatican gallery.

In the Vatican gallery, in Rome, Will Ladislaw and his friend, Adolf Naumann, a young German artist, observe Dorothea. Despite the fact that she is 'clad in Quakerish grey drapery' (p. 189), Naumann admires her, taking special note of her beautiful hands. Ladislaw, clearly ruffled, identifies her as the wife of his second cousin. Naumann, who wants Dorothea to model for a painting, perceives that Ladislaw is jealous of Casaubon.

COMMENTARY

The scene shifts from Middlemarch to Rome. Dorothea's chaste clothing looks even more out of place amid the richness of this city. Ladislaw is accustomed to European travel. His cosmopolitan outlook contrasts with the narrow provincialism of Dorothea's upbringing. His friendship with a German artist confirms his affinity with **Romantic** aesthetics and philosophy. His knowledge of contemporary German culture allows him a perspective upon Casaubon's work which will soon prove revelatory and shocking to Dorothea.

CONTEXT

The **epigraph** is from the *Purgatory* section of *The Divine Comedy*, a three-part epic by Italian poet Dante Alighieri (c. 1265–1321). It means, 'See the other, who, sighing, has made a bed for her cheek with the palm of her hand'. Eliot has altered the gender of the grieving figure who, in the original, is a man.

GLOSSARY

188	the most brilliant English critic of the day William Hazlitt (1778–1830), essayist
188	certain long-haired German artists at Rome reference to a group known as the Nazarenes
188	Meleager hunter in Greek mythology
188	Ariadne daughter of King Minos of Crete. She used a ball of thread to assist the escape of Theseus from the labyrinth, after he had killed the Minotaur

189	*Geistlicher* (German) clergyman
190	*Antigone* in Greek myth, the daughter of Oedipus. A model of filial devotion
191	*Der Neffe als Onkel* comedy by the German dramatist Schiller (1803)
191	*ungeheuer* (German) monstrous

CHAPTER 20

- Dorothea feels neglected by her husband. She offers to assist with his work, but her remarks anger him.

Dorothea offers to assist preparation of a text for publication from her husband's copious notes. Casaubon responds with anger to her comments regarding the inconclusive state of his work, and Dorothea becomes indignant in turn. She tries to effect reconciliation, and goes with him to the Vatican. It is after Casaubon has left her for the library that Naumann first observes her, as recorded in the previous chapter.

Two hours later, Dorothea sits sobbing in her room. She has been in Rome for five weeks. Casaubon has buried himself in study at the Vatican library, and his young wife from provincial Middlemarch feels isolated in the strange old city. Her perception of marriage to Casaubon has undergone dramatic revision.

COMMENTARY

Dorothea's discontent grows as the 'stupendous fragmentariness of the ancient city heightens the dreamlike strangeness of her bridal life' (p. 192). She feels out of place amongst Rome's 'ruins and basilicas, palaces and colossi' (p. 193). The landscape and architecture suggest a **metaphor** appropriate to describe her changing perception of Casaubon: 'the large vistas and wide fresh air which she had dreamed of finding in her husband's mind were

CONTEXT

The Vatican art gallery visited by the Casaubons is quite distinct from the current building fulfilling that function, which was inaugurated in 1932. The collection they visited had only been open to the public since 1817 when, following Napoleon's fall from power, confiscated paintings were restored to the Catholic Church.

 CHECK THE BOOK

Dorothea's honeymoon in Rome is an austere and depressing affair. Compare this to the depiction of Rome as a highly romantic yet potentially dangerous place for a young woman to visit in the novella *Daisy Miller* (1878) by American novelist Henry James (1843–1916).

replaced by ante-rooms and winding passages which seemed to lead nowhither' (p. 195).

This chapter contains a sequence comparable to cinematic **flashback**, recounting earlier events in order to cast light on the circumstances which resulted in Dorothea's presence at the Vatican gallery.

CHAPTER 21

- Ladislaw visits Dorothea in her apartment. He sees that she has been weeping. They discuss Casaubon's work.
- Casaubon returns from his studies.

Dorothea stops sobbing when Tantripp, her maid, announces the arrival of a gentleman, related to Casaubon, who wishes to see her. Ladislaw reveals that he saw her earlier in the Vatican museum. He recognises that she has been weeping, and feels appalled at the thought of Casaubon spending his honeymoon 'groping after his mouldy futilities' (p. 205). He talks of painting, and then discusses her husband's work, suggesting that new scholarship in Germany has rendered those labours obsolete. Casaubon arrives home and, making it clear he is too tired for company, invites Ladislaw to dinner the following day.

COMMENTARY

The circumstances of Dorothea's honeymoon lead Ladislaw to feel 'a sort of comic disgust' (p. 205). The word 'disgust' links his reaction to those of Celia and Chettam upon learning of the engagement.

CHAPTER 22

- Ladislaw dines with Mr and Mrs Casaubon.
- The following day he conducts them around artists' studios. Naumann sketches the couple.
- The next day, Ladislaw visits Dorothea when she is alone, and laments the conditions of her marriage. He affirms that Casaubon's scholarship is outmoded and determines to live independently of his cousin.

Casaubon and Dorothea find Ladislaw an agreeable dinner guest, and it is agreed that he will conduct them to artists' studios the following day. They visit the painter Naumann, and Ladislaw shows them some of his own sketches. Naumann asks Casaubon to sit for him, as his head will be perfect for his painting of St Thomas Aquinas. He seizes the opportunity to sketch Dorothea, in the pose of Santa Clara.

Left alone, the two young men mock Casaubon's self-centredness, and extol the beauty of his wife. Ladislaw desires to see Dorothea alone, in order to make a more emphatic impression on her. He visits around noon the following day, when her husband is out. Dorothea is choosing cameo jewellery for Celia. Ladislaw speaks with passion against Dorothea's cloistered life. She asserts that Lowick Manor is her chosen home.

Ladislaw's remarks about the shortcomings in Casaubon's work make Dorothea angry, and he announces his intention to return to England and live independently of Casaubon's financial support. He declares he will not see Dorothea again. They speak with evident warmth for one another, and tears appear in their eyes.

Departing, Ladislaw encounters Casaubon and they exchange farewells. That evening Dorothea tells her husband of Ladislaw's resolve to live independently. Casaubon responds with cold uninterest. He asks Dorothea to desist from further mention of Ladislaw.

CONTEXT

The epigraph is a stanza from the poem 'Une bonne Fortune' written in 1834 by Alfred de Musset (1810–57): 'We talked for a long time; she was straightforward and kind. / Not knowing evil, she did what was good; / She made a gift to me of the riches of her heart, / And listening as she gave her heart to me, / Without daring to think, I gave her mine; / She carried away my life without even knowing that she did so.'

CONTEXT

Saint Clare (1194–1253) (or Santa Clara) founded an enclosed monastic order for women, now commonly referred to as the Poor Clares. The order renounces worldly pleasures and is devoted to manual labour and prayer.

CHECK THE NET

St Thomas Aquinas (*c.* 1225–74) was an Italian priest and philosopher, whose writings exerted enormous influence upon the development of theology and the history of the Catholic Church. An image of Aquinas can be found at **http://www. english.upenn. edu.** Search for 'Aquinas'.

QUESTION

In 1879 the novelist W. H. Mallock declared that George Eliot was 'the first great godless writer of fiction that has appeared in England'. She regarded herself as agnostic rather than atheist, however. What traces of belief in God's existence do you find in *Middlemarch*?

COMMENTARY

In the early days of their acquaintance, Dorothea frequently compared Casaubon to eminent men such as Locke, Milton, and Pascal. She is delighted when Naumann asks her husband to act as a model for his portrait of Aquinas. Neither she nor her husband recognises the mockery of the invitation, which is really an excuse for the artist to spend time in Dorothea's company. It is characteristic of Casaubon's self-centredness that he arranges to buy the flattering portrait of himself, but shows little interest in the depiction of his wife.

Ladislaw remarks that scholarship in Casaubon's field is 'as changing as chemistry: new discoveries are constantly making new points of view' (pp. 221–2). George Eliot was acutely aware of changes wrought in all fields of knowledge as the nineteenth century unfolded. Ladislaw identifies a process which was to result in widespread anxiety in European culture as old and comforting certainties gave way to new and unfamiliar interpretations.

GLOSSARY

212	**Middleton** Conyers Middleton (1682–1750), theological controversialist
213	**Thorwaldsen** Bertel Thorwaldsen (1770–1844), Danish sculptor based in Rome
214	*pfuscherei* (German) bungling
220	**Minotaurs** in Greek myth, the minotaur had the head of a bull and the body of a man
222	**Paracelsus** pseudonym of Theophrastus Bombastus von Hohenheim (1493–1541), Swiss physician
222	**Bryant** Jacob Bryant (1715–1804), author of *An Analysis of Ancient Mythology*
222	**Cush and Mizraim** sons of Ham, who was a son of Noah
224	*porte cochère* (French) carriage entrance

CHAPTER 23

- On account of his debts, Fred Vincy decides to sell his horse to raise cash, but buys another at greater expense.

Fred Vincy owes one hundred and sixty pounds to Bambridge, a local horse-dealer. Fred is optimistic about prospects for settling the debt, for which Caleb Garth acted as security. Mrs Vincy fears an engagement between her son and Mary Garth, who have been close friends since childhood.

Featherstone's gift of one hundred pounds fell short of Fred's immediate financial requirements, and he determines to sell his horse in order to raise money. After retrieving the eighty pounds entrusted to his mother, Fred rides to Houndsley horse-fair. On the way, at the Red Lion inn, Fred exchanges his horse plus thirty pounds for a grey horse called Diamond, which he hopes to sell to Lord Medlicote for eighty pounds.

COMMENTARY

Debt is an important factor in the plot of *Middlemarch*. Financial debts are a clear measure of dependency upon others. Fred endures the humiliation administered by Featherstone because he hopes to inherit money from him. On the other hand, his unsettled debts will have repercussions for the kindly Garth family. Lydgate develops substantial debts later in the novel, and as a consequence becomes entangled with Bulstrode's fate. Economic relationships of this kind illustrate that nobody lives in isolation, and that individual characters are inevitably caught up in a web of dependencies and responsibilities.

CONTEXT

Debt was a serious social problem during the nineteenth century. Charles Dickens (1812–70), whose own father, John, was imprisoned for debt, made it an important issue in his fiction. It's a constant threat for the memorable Wilkins Micawber in *David Copperfield* (1850), and the grim shadow of Marshalsea debtors' prison, where John Dickens was incarcerated, looms large in *Little Dorrit* (1857).

GLOSSARY

232	**Lindley Murray** author of *English Grammar* (1795)
232	**Mangnall's *Questions*** Mrs Richmal Mangnall's *Historical and Miscellaneous Questions* (1800), a standard school textbook continued

233	'cute acute or shrewd
233	jockies horse-dealers
237	blacklegs swindlers at horse-racing
238	roarer horse that breathes heavily

CONTEXT

The **epigraph** is from 'Sonnet XXIV' by William Shakespeare (1564–1616). Note how Shakespeare's use of the word 'cross' implies that Christ's suffering was the **type** of all human suffering.

CONTEXT

With the passing of the Elementary Education Act in 1870 free and compulsory education was provided for all children in England. Before that, schooling was largely unregulated and depended upon less formal provision such as the so-called 'Dame schools' run by women like Mrs Garth, in their own homes (p. 243).

CHAPTER 24

- Fred's new horse injures itself.
- He admits to Caleb Garth that he is unable to pay his debts. Money set aside for the education of Garth's son Alfred will be used for that purpose.

The horse, Diamond, proves to be wild and injures itself. The debt has to be settled soon, and Fred has only fifty pounds left. He rides to the Garth family's old fashioned, rambling house, and finds Mrs Garth doing housework, while providing education for her children, Letty and Ben. She tells Fred that she has only one other pupil at present to add to her income.

Caleb Garth arrives home. Fred reveals his financial plight. Mrs Garth was previously unaware of her husband's involvement with the debt. He is too short of money to help, but his wife offers savings reserved for their son Alfred's education. Mary will be able to provide the remainder.

Her kindness touches Fred with remorse. He departs feeling extremely uncomfortable. Susan Garth expresses her disappointment with Fred, and agrees with her husband's view that he himself has acted foolishly. She tells him to desist from his habit of working without payment.

COMMENTARY

Education is another major concern in *Middlemarch*. George Eliot does not idealise learning: Casaubon's erudition proves sterile; Lydgate experiences serious problems despite his specialist knowledge. Nonetheless, education clearly plays its part in the author's conception of the general development of society. Women in nineteenth-century England were denied access to educational opportunities open to men, and that is reflected in the very different experiences of Dorothea and of Rosamond.

Mrs Garth unquestioningly endorses the view that women are 'framed to be entirely subordinate' (p. 243). She accepts that men are socially superior. Her son Christy is at university, and it was intended that his brother Alfred should follow him. But she is content for her daughter Mary to act as a servant to Featherstone (see **Themes: The role of women**).

> **GLOSSARY**
>
> 243 **the Subjunctive Mood** in traditional grammar, the mode of verbs in sentences expressing doubt, wishes or regrets
>
> 243 **the Torrid Zone** region of the earth between the tropics

CHAPTER 25

- Fred reveals to Mary Garth the position in which he has placed her parents. She is furious.
- Fred leaves, feeling ill.
- Garth visits his daughter to borrow money from her.

Fred rides to Stone Court and tells Mary of his debt, and of the position in which her father has been placed. Mary cries, furious that her parents should now face such difficulties. Despite her anger, she manages to feel pity for Fred. After paying a short visit to Featherstone, Fred departs, feeling unwell.

Soon after dusk, Caleb Garth arrives at Stone Court. After brief discussion with Featherstone, he talks with Mary about his obligation to settle the debt. Garth advises his daughter not to

> **CONTEXT**
>
> The epigraph is from *Songs of Experience* (1794) by William Blake (1757–1827). The poems in this collection are concerned with the loss of innocence that invariably comes with our exposure to the ways of the world.

become entangled in Fred's future. Mary assures him, 'I will never engage myself to one who has no manly independence, and who goes on loitering away his time on the chance that others will provide for him' (p. 257). Taking eighteen pounds from her, Garth leaves Mary alone with Featherstone.

COMMENTARY

Mary Garth does not have the beauty of Rosamond, nor the aspirations of Dorothea. She is plain, and she applies herself to practical tasks with exemplary common sense. But she has a rare capacity for sympathy, which is evident even here, when Fred has wronged her family. In a novel peopled with characters who are blinkered by selfishness, Mary's altruism provides a telling contrast (see **Themes: Altruism and egotism**).

Mary is not an idealised character, however. One of her failings, which she has in common with her mother, is a ready acceptance of female subordination.

GLOSSARY

252 **Mrs Piozzi's recollections of Johnson** Hester Lynch Piozzi published Anecdotes of the late Samuel Johnson, in 1786

CHAPTER 26

CONTEXT

The **epigraph** is spoken by Thersites, a Greek soldier and a rogue, in William Shakespeare's play Troilus and Cressida, Act II Scene 3.

- Fred's illness intensifies.
- Lydgate attends him, and diagnoses typhoid.

Fred feels unwell, and asks his mother to send for Mr Wrench, a doctor, who assures them the illness is not serious. Next morning the fever, contracted in the unsanitary streets of Houndsley, has intensified. Rosamond notices Lydgate passing their house, and her mother asks for his help. Lydgate diagnoses typhoid and prescribes a suitable course of treatment.

COMMENTARY

This chapter presents a dramatic rendering of the conflict between old and new medical practices, as exemplified by Wrench and Lydgate. Wrench shares his name with an old fashioned surgical implement used for putting mechanical pressure upon deformed bones. The name indicates clearly that he lacks the subtlety of Lydgate's scientific approach. Within the novel Lydgate's reforming zeal achieves very little in practical terms, but George Eliot understood that change has to overcome resistance, and is invariably achieved through gradual evolution.

CHAPTER 27

- Fred's health steadily improves.
- Romance develops between Rosamond and Lydgate.

The younger Vincys are sent away on account of Fred's illness. Rosamond remains with her parents, and she and Lydgate are brought 'within effective proximity' (p. 264). As Fred steadily improves, a message from Featherstone arrives, announcing that the old man has missed Fred's visits. Fred is upset not to have heard from Mary.

The 'mutual fascination' (p. 266) between Lydgate and Rosamond persists after normality has been restored to the house. Lydgate, who lacks money and is dedicated to research, does not intend to marry for several years. Rosamond, on the other hand, eagerly anticipates their marriage, and 'a handsome house' (p. 267). Lydgate's evident success with Rosamond arouses hostility amongst rivals for her affection, including Ned Plymdale, a young man regarded in Middlemarch as a worthwhile suitor despite his intellectual limitations. Lydgate is summoned to attend at Lowick Manor.

COMMENTARY

Middlemarch is subtitled 'A Study of Provincial Life', and the narrowness of experience this implies is one of the novel's major concerns. Limited horizons breed false expectations; this is the case with Rosamond's view of Lydgate, as it is with Dorothea's view of

CONTEXT

Typhoid fever is spread by bacteria in water or food contaminated by sewage. It caused major health problems in crowded and poorly sanitised cities and towns in Victorian Britain.

 CHECK THE BOOK

During the nineteenth century there was a major shift of population from rural areas to towns and cities, which grew overcrowded and insanitary as a consequence. As a provincial community, Middlemarch stands on the cusp between life in the countryside and new urban conditions. Raymond Williams's *The Country and The City* (Chatto & Windus, 1985; 1973) is a classic study of issues raised by such demographic shifts over the centuries. In the course of his broad discussion Williams makes reference to George Eliot's earlier fiction.

GLOSSARY

269 **Keepsake**
fashionable literary
annual

270 **Lady
Blessington**
Marguerite, Countess
of Blessington
(1789–1849), novelist
who edited The
Keepsake

270 **L.E.L.** Letitia
Elizabeth Landon
(1803–38), poet and
novelist

Casaubon. In both relationships the young women anticipate that marriage will grant access to a new and fulfilling world. Lydgate's relative urbanity is emphasised through contrast with the provincial outlook of Rosamond's other suitor, Ned Plymdale.

The summons to Lowick Manor is indicative of Lydgate's growing reputation. It also signals convergence between the two main strands of the story. The circumstances which resulted in the summons are described in Chapter 29.

CHAPTER 28

- The Casaubons return home.
- Mr Casaubon is unwell.

The Casaubons return to Lowick Manor in mid January. Casaubon gets up early, complaining of heart palpitations. Later, Celia and her uncle arrive. Brooke notes Casaubon's paleness. Celia tells Dorothea of her engagement to Sir James Chettam.

COMMENTARY

Middlemarch's provincial nature is again highlighted here. Following her exposure to the wider world, Lowick seems altogether less consequential to Dorothea. Her expectation of active involvement in her husband's intellectual endeavours has also diminished. She now inhabits 'a pale fantastic world that seemed to be vanishing from the daylight' (p. 274). She remains ardent in her desire for a more fulfilling life, but her existence seems to have become 'a nightmare in which every object was withering and shrinking away from her' (p. 275).

The portrait of Casaubon's aunt Julia starts to exercise a strange fascination for Dorothea, explicable in part because she is said to have made an unfortunate marriage, but also because this woman was the grandmother of Will Ladislaw, the young man who has awakened Dorothea's emotional life. Meanwhile, her devoted attention to Casaubon has waned to the point where others recognise in her husband 'signs which she had not noticed' (p. 276).

CHAPTER 29

- A letter from Ladislaw annoys Casaubon who, soon afterwards, suffers a heart attack.
- Lydgate attends to him.

CONTEXT

The **epigraph** is from *The Vicar of Wakefield* (1766), a novel of rural life by Oliver Goldsmith (c. 1730–74).

Several weeks later, Dorothea joins her husband in the library, where he is at work. Casaubon gives her a letter from Ladislaw. It was enclosed with another, addressed to him, in which Ladislaw proposed to visit Lowick. Casaubon intends to decline that proposal on the grounds that he is too busy to be distracted by the younger man's 'desultory vivacity' (p. 282). Dorothea reacts angrily, and turns resentfully to the copying work Casaubon has allocated to her, leaving the letter from Ladislaw unread.

After half an hour, she is startled by the sound of a book falling and finds Casaubon in physical distress, struggling to breathe. She assists him with tender concern. Arriving to discover Casaubon lying on a couch, slowly reviving, and Dorothea recovering from her shock, Chettam recommends that they send for Lydgate. The doctor soon comes, and attends to the couple. Chettam and Celia lament Dorothea's marriage to Casaubon.

COMMENTARY

George Eliot involves us directly with two of the novel's main concerns: point of view, and the capacity to extend sympathy to others. At the same time, it is evident that the points of view of Casaubon and Dorothea are growing further apart, and that the capacity for sympathy between them is accordingly diminished. Moreover, despite Casaubon's illness he is not regarded sympathetically by Celia, who says she 'never did like him', nor by Chettam, who considers the marriage 'a horrible sacrifice' of Dorothea (p. 284).

The arrival of Lydgate to attend to Casaubon is continuous with the end of Chapter 27.

CHAPTER 30

- Lydgate alerts Dorothea to the possibility that her husband might die suddenly.
- She asks her uncle to deter a visit from Ladislaw, but Brooke invites the young man to call on him at Tipton Grange.

It is March. Immediate danger to Casaubon has passed, but Lydgate continues to attend to him and advises that he should work less. Lydgate tells Dorothea that Casaubon is almost restored to his usual state of health, but recommends watchfulness. He says her husband might live fifteen years or more. On the other hand, death might occur suddenly. Casaubon should be kept as free from anxiety as possible.

Dorothea is deeply affected by this news and appeals to Lydgate for help and advice. She struggles to remain outwardly calm but is turbulent inside. Once alone, she cries. Composing herself, she reads Ladislaw's letters. He intends to make his way in life independently. At a convenient time, he will visit Lowick to deliver Naumann's picture, featuring Casaubon as Aquinas.

She asks her uncle to contact Ladislaw, informing him that Casaubon's illness precludes such a visit. In the course of writing, however, Brooke invites Ladislaw to visit him at Tipton Grange. He envisages that Ladislaw's talents might assist his own political ambition.

COMMENTARY

We are told that Dorothea's request for assistance stayed with Lydgate for years, a 'cry from soul to soul, without other consciousness than their moving with kindred natures in the same embroiled medium, the same troublous fitfully-illuminated

GLOSSARY

279 **Parerga**
secondary works

281 **Brasenose**
college of Oxford University

281 **Warburton's**
William Warburton (1698–1779), bishop

281 *viros nullo aevo perituros* (Latin) men who will never pass away

CONTEXT

The **epigraph** is from Pascal's *Pensées* (Thoughts) and means, 'he who relaxes aimlessly tires himself'. Pascal is named in Chapter 1 as one of the authors Dorothea reads.

life' (p. 290). This elevated description conveys the high seriousness with which both characters view the world and their role in it. They are in certain ways parallel figures, sharing high aspirations and meeting with bitter disappointments.

> **GLOSSARY**
>
> 286 **Smollett** Tobias Smollett (1721–71), Scottish novelist

CHAPTER 31

- Fred Vincy recuperates at Stone Court.
- Lydgate and Rosamond become engaged.

In order to recuperate, Fred Vincy stays for a while at Stone Court. His mother goes with him, eager to prevent his engagement to Mary Garth. Mrs Bulstrode pays regular visits to her brother, Vincy, in his wife's absence. Ned Plymdale's mother has alerted Mrs Bulstrode to the intimacy growing between Rosamond and Lydgate. She challenges her niece directly. Rosamond denies entering into a secret engagement. Her aunt cautions that Lydgate is poor. Rosamond responds with reference to the doctor's good family connections. Mrs Bulstrode speaks favourably of Ned Plymdale as a potential husband.

Mr Bulstrode is pressed by his wife to enquire after Lydgate's intentions. The doctor declares he has no intention of marrying. Mrs Bulstrode then speaks directly with Lydgate. The doctor is disturbed by this intrusion into his affairs, and resolves to visit the Vincys only when business necessitates.

Visiting Stone Court, Lydgate is asked by Mrs Vincy to report to her husband a decline in Featherstone's health, and to request that he visit the old man. Lydgate finds Rosamond alone. Both are embarrassed, and his forced formality upsets her. She cries; he kisses her. He asks her to be his wife, and she accepts. Lydgate returns that evening and Mr Vincy grants his approval of the engagement. Vincy, aware of the imminent demise of Featherstone, is buoyant at the prospect of Fred's likely inheritance, and he grants assent without hesitation.

> **CONTEXT**
>
> In this chapter George Eliot **alludes** to 'sirens' (p. 299), enchantresses in Greek myth, who sang to lure sailors to their death, and to 'Ariadne' (p. 299), a woman deserted in another Greek myth by Theseus after she had rescued him from imprisonment in a labyrinth (see also Chapter 19). Such allusions broaden the novel's scope of reference to relationships between men and women. They might also remind us of the **paradox** that Casaubon has pursued a life of austere study on the basis of such passionate tales.

COMMENTARY

Lydgate's declaration that he prefers to tend the poor rather than the wealthy indicates his selfless dedication to the profession of medicine, untainted by material considerations. It does not bode well for his marriage to the materialistic Rosamond.

We are told that Rosamond has 'a great sense of being a romantic heroine, and playing the part prettily' (p. 297). This not only suggests her superficiality, but also recalls the actress with whom Lydgate was infatuated in Paris, and who killed her own husband. George Eliot avoids presenting Rosamond as a villain, however; rather, she is a victim of narrow horizons imposed by patriarchal assumptions. She has been made vain and shallow by her education and her stereotypical femininity.

CONTEXT

The **epigraph** is taken from a speech by Prospero's brother Antonio, the treacherous Duke of Milan, in Act II Scene 1 of Shakespeare's *The Tempest*.

CHAPTER 32

- Featherstone's relatives gather as his health deteriorates.

Featherstone's blood relations are agitated at the prospect of his imminent demise. They become intensely watchful of one another, and of other possible claimants. The old man refuses to see these visitors. Some linger in the kitchen, where Mary Garth finds herself under constant scrutiny.

Featherstone's brother Solomon, and his sister, Jane Waule, suspect that their brother has left money to Mary. They are outraged to find Mrs Vincy and Fred in the old man's company, while they are rebuffed. The auctioneer, Borthrop Trumbull, who is to be a bearer at the funeral, is also allowed to visit the old man.

COMMENTARY

Featherstone's relatives appear comically grotesque in their self-centredness, but their greed, envy, and lack of sympathy for the

CONTEXT

Mrs Waule's reference to 'Blue-Coat land' (p. 311) **alludes** to charity schools where pupils wore long blue coats. Some of these institutions date back to the sixteenth century and still exist today.

dying man are really just extreme depictions of qualities exhibited by more central figures in the novel. At the start of Chapter 31, for example, Rosamond remarks that Dorothea is 'of course' devoted to Casaubon, 'but she was thinking at the same time that it was not so very melancholy to be mistress of Lowick Manor with a husband likely to die soon' (p. 293). The grasping materialism implied by Rosamond's thoughts contrasts starkly with Dorothea's idealistic aspirations.

GLOSSARY

305 **Brobdingnag** land of giants in Jonathan Swift's *Gulliver's Travels* (1726)

305 **Borrow** George Borrow (1803–81), writer

CHAPTER 33

- Mary Garth attends Featherstone. He asks her to destroy his most recent will, but she refuses.
- The old man dies.

CONTEXT

The epigraph is spoken by King Henry in Act III Scene 3 of Shakespeare's play *King Henry VI, Part 2* (c. 1590).

From midnight, Mary Garth watches over Peter Featherstone. She smiles at the follies of the day, but is concerned that the Vincys might be disappointed in their expectation of a substantial inheritance. At three in the morning, Featherstone asks her to destroy one of the two wills he has made, which are locked in an iron chest. Mary refuses adamantly, despite his offer of money and gold. The old man cries like a child. Soon afterwards he dies.

COMMENTARY

Mary's scrupulous concern not to be seen to act dishonourably for personal gain contrasts starkly with the greed of Featherstone's predatory relatives. Her decision is not an isolated event; its repercussions will shape the lives of other characters as the story unfolds.

CHAPTER 34

CONTEXT

Handloom
weavers were,
around 1830,
amongst the
poorest members
of the English
working class.
The German
sociologist
Friedrich Engels
(1820–95), in *The
Condition of the
Working Class in
England in 1844*,
wrote
metaphorically of
middle class
manufacturers as
capitalist vampires
who thrived on
life-blood
extracted from
their workers.

GLOSSARY

323 **Harpagon** a
miser in Molière's play
The Miser (1668)

329 *omne tulit
punctum* (Latin) he
carried every point

330 **Hobbes** Thomas
Hobbes (1588–1679),
philosopher

- Featherstone's funeral takes place.
- Dorothea is alarmed to see Ladislaw in the attendant crowd.

Peter Featherstone is buried in accordance with his instructions for an elaborate funeral, conducted by Cadwallader. The rector's wife, Lady Chettam, Dorothea, and Celia watch the occasion from an upper window in Casaubon's house. Brooke arrives. Casaubon joins the group just before Celia spots Ladislaw below. Another man, a stranger 'described by Mrs Cadwallader as frog-faced' (p. 332), is also noticed. News of Ladislaw's arrival shocks Dorothea, who turns pale. Brooke explains that the young man is staying as his guest. Casaubon suspects that his wife has invited Ladislaw, despite the fact that he has forbidden her to do so. Brooke volunteers to fetch his guest, who has brought with him Naumann's painting of Casaubon.

COMMENTARY

The physical setting, with the Chettams, Brookes, and Mrs Cadwallader looking down upon those from lower social classes, reminds us of the traditional stratification of English society. The hierarchy is undergoing change with the relentless march of the middle classes.

In Chapter 16, George Eliot makes overt reference to 'a sort of vampire's feast' (p. 156). Here she has the upper class character Mrs Cadwallader describe the middle class manufacturer Mr Vincy as 'one of those who suck the life out of the wretched handloom weavers in Tipton and Freshitt' (p. 327). The **metaphor** once again suggests a vampire's feast.

CHAPTER 35

- Both wills are read.
- Joshua Rigg inherits the estate. Fred receives nothing.

There is jealous rivalry amongst those who attend the funeral, all expectant of some share in the legacy. They assemble for the will to be read, and are disturbed by the presence of the frog-faced stranger. He is in his early thirties, and his name is Joshua Rigg. Mary Garth has seen him twice at Stone Court.

Standish, the lawyer, reads the will he drew up for Featherstone in 1825. Ten thousand pounds is bequeathed to Fred. The bulk of the remaining property and land goes to Rigg. But Standish then reads a second will, drawn up by another lawyer in 1826, with a codicil added in 1828. There is great agitation; only Rigg remains perfectly calm. He retains his legacy, and is henceforth to take the name Featherstone. The money Fred expected to receive will be used to build alms-houses for the elderly poor. Trumbull receives a gold headed cane. The relatives bitterly bemoan their lot. Rigg coolly talks business with Standish.

Mary Garth is aware that by refusing to destroy the second will at Featherstone's command, she has blighted Fred Vincy's fortunes. Both she and he now need employment.

COMMENTARY

Middlemarch is crucially concerned with frustrated expectations. This chapter shows such expectations at their most crude and materialistic. Compared to this predatory gathering the aspirations of Dorothea and Lydgate seem all the more elevated.

The **narrator** who began the novel musing on St Theresa is now discussing Joshua Rigg, Featherstone's illegitimate son. There is self-conscious reflection 'on the means of elevating a low subject' (p. 341). It is recommended that the account be regarded as a **parable**. This is **ironic**; *Middlemarch* is a complex work of literary

CONTEXT

The **epigraph** is derived from the play *Le Légataire Universel* (1708) by French comic dramatist Jean-François Regnard (1655–1709). It means: 'No, I know of no pleasure more charming than to see the inheritors at the reading of a lengthy will – an afflicted gang with their disconcerted bearing and long faces, pallid and appalled. One bids them goodnight, thumbing one's nose. I would return, I think, from the next world in order to witness their deep sadness.'

GLOSSARY

332 **batrachian**
frog-like

341 **loobies**
clownish figures

realism, not a vehicle for simple parables. George Eliot seems here to be indicating that as an artist she is committed to reflecting the wide spectrum of human nature, rather than presenting an idealised depiction of the world.

CHAPTER 36

CONTEXT

The **epigraph** is from the poetic drama *The Tragedy of Philotas* (1605) by Samuel Daniel (1562–1619). This again indicates the breadth of George Eliot's reading.

- Plans for Rosamond's marriage to Lydgate go ahead, despite Mr and Mrs Vincy's uneasiness about the doctor's financial prospects.

Mr Vincy presses Fred to return to university and pass his exams. He laments Rosamond's engagement to Lydgate, who has family connections but no money, and he vows he will oppose their marriage. Fred is faced with the prospect of having to make his own way in life. Rosamond, on the other hand, refuses to take her father's position seriously. He proves malleable to her influence, and recognises that it is too late to intervene.

Mrs Bulstrode speaks out against the match, but Vincy replies that it was her husband's trust in Lydgate that prompted his own amenability to him. Bulstrode himself laments to his wife that Lydgate has become involved with a girl who is 'obstinately worldly' (p. 347).

Lydgate receives a visit from Farebrother, who wishes to use his microscope. Lydgate suggests that the stability of marriage should assist his work, although secretly he looks forward to escaping from the demands of courtship, which he considers futile.

GLOSSARY

346 **Santa Lucia**
third-century martyr, associated with cures for eye defects

354 **Valenciennes**
fine lace

He suggests to Rosamond that they should marry in six weeks time, arranges to take a house she likes, and buys an expensive dinner service. Rosamond, who is socially ambitious, is anxious to visit Lydgate's uncle Godwin at his Quallingham estate. Lydgate is offended by Mrs Vincy's suggestion that his uncle might give the couple money, but manages to conceal his distaste.

COMMENTARY

In Christian terms, Providence refers to God's all-encompassing plan for the world. In *Middlemarch*, the word 'providence' recurs as a secular concept, indicating a naive faith that things will, of necessity, turn out well. Before the reading of the will, Fred Vincy believed in 'providence in the shape of an old gentleman's caprice' (p. 343). Now, he is faced with the need to take responsibility for his own life.

For all his progressive ideas about medical practice, Lydgate is generally conservative by temperament, and his views on gender are steeped in patriarchal assumptions. The **narrator** remarks that 'Lydgate relied much on the psychological difference between what for the sake of variety I will call goose and gander: especially the innate submissiveness of the goose as beautifully corresponding to the strength of the gander' (p. 356).

CHAPTER 37

- Brooke buys a reforming newspaper and appoints Ladislaw editor.
- Ladislaw speaks with Dorothea alone, and the bond of sympathy between them grows.
- Casaubon writes to his cousin instructing him to leave the area. Ladislaw refuses to comply.

Mr Brooke has bought the *Pioneer* newspaper, in order to press the case for Reform and, to Casaubon's annoyance, has engaged Ladislaw to edit it. Ladislaw feels with increasing intensity that Casaubon has wronged Dorothea by marrying her.

One day, Ladislaw is sketching at Lowick, hoping to encounter Dorothea walking. Rain drives him to seek shelter at her home. She is alone in the library, and welcomes him with 'the simple sincerity of an unhappy child visited at school' (p. 362). As they talk, he

CONTEXT

Chapter 37 **alludes** to the dissolution of Parliament and an imminent election. The reforming politician Lord John Russell (1792–1878) introduced the Reform Bill into the Commons in March 1831. It sought to address corruption in the electoral system but was defeated in April and Parliament was dissolved. Earl Grey was then returned as Prime Minister. The Reform Act was eventually passed in 1832, introducing wide-ranging changes to the parliamentary system.

CONTEXT

The epigraph is a **sonnet** from the cycle of courtship poems *Amoretti* (1595) by the Elizabethan Poet Laureate, Edmund Spenser (c. 1552–99).

William Huskisson (1770–1830) (p. 358), a Member of Parliament and cautious supporter of Reform, is now remembered mostly as the first person to be killed in a railway accident. He was fatally injured when he walked in front of the famous 'Rocket' steam engine, driven by its inventor George Stephenson (1781–1848), during the inaugural journey of the Liverpool and Manchester Railway. This accident is mentioned in Chapter 41 (p. 416).

comprehends that she has married in order to assist the scholarly Casaubon with his work.

Ladislaw tells Dorothea about his grandmother who was disowned by Casaubon's family, and about her husband, a Polish patriot who made his living by teaching. He also speaks of his father, who died young, and of his mother who ran away from her family in order to go on stage. Casaubon financially supported Ladislaw and his mother, who died four years previously.

Ladislaw discusses his arrangement with Brooke and his desire to stay in Middlemarch. He departs before his cousin returns home, and Dorothea raises the matter on his behalf. Casaubon writes a letter indicating that if Ladislaw does not comply with his request to withdraw from the area he will no longer be welcome at Lowick Manor. Dorothea, meanwhile, forms a strong sense of the injustice with which Ladislaw's grandmother was treated on account of her marriage to a poor man.

The Casaubons awaken early the next morning. Dorothea suggests that her own money and property are excessive to her needs, and proposes that she offer Ladislaw assistance. Casaubon is furious. She experiences 'a dumb inward cry for help to bear this nightmare of a life in which every energy was arrested by dread' (p. 375).

The next day, a letter arrives from Ladislaw telling Casaubon that he does not share his view of the situation. He acknowledges indebtedness for past support, but denies that this enables Casaubon to curb his freedom. Casaubon receives the message in silence, but his bitterness towards Ladislaw grows.

COMMENTARY

This is a crucial chapter for the development of a bond of sympathy between Dorothea and Ladislaw. He is aggrieved at her unsuitable marriage. She wishes to make amends for his grandmother's exclusion from Casaubon's family, on account of a marriage perceived as unsuitable. Casaubon, on the other hand, seeks to exclude Ladislaw. The young man's refusal to be dictated to intensifies Casaubon's bitterness, which will later culminate in the codicil appended to his will.

GLOSSARY

357	Charles James Fox (1749–1806), reforming politician
358	dark-blue freemen dark blue was the colour associated with the Liberal party. Freemen were able to vote in parliamentary elections
361	Sir Thomas Browne (1605–82), physician and author of *Religio Medici* (1642) and other works. Widely regarded as one of the finest writers on English prose
361	Delectus anthology of Greek or Latin passages for translation
373	Lowth probably Robert Lowth (1710–87), bishop, scholar, and poet

---

CHAPTER 38

- Chettam and the Cadwalladers seek to deter Brooke from his political activities.

Chettam has lunch with the Cadwalladers. They disparage Brooke's reformist political activities. Ladislaw's cleverness is acknowledged, although he is regarded locally with suspicion, as 'a quill-driving alien, a foreign emissary' (p. 379). Mrs Cadwallader calls him 'a Byronic hero' and 'a dangerous young sprig' (p. 380).

Chettam criticises the management of Brooke's estate and bemoans the loss of Dorothea's salutary influence at Tipton Grange. Brooke's tenants have been neglected since he dismissed the admirable Caleb Garth, twelve years previously. Brooke drops in, only to depart unsettled, following a concerted effort to persuade him of his folly.

COMMENTARY

George Eliot shifts the focus onto a discussion amongst less central characters. This is a way of controlling levels of emotional intensity

CONTEXT

Translated, the **epigraph** reads: 'Men plentifully pass judgement upon human actions; sooner or later some good must come of it.' The quotation is from the eminent French historian and politician François Guizot (1787–1874).

CONTEXT

A 'Byronic hero' is a **type** resembling George Gordon, Lord Byron (1788–1824), an aristocratic **Romantic** poet who became a celebrity during the nineteenth century on account of his dashing and extravagant lifestyle.

GLOSSARY

381 **modus** money paid in lieu of a tithe

382 **Lafitte** Jacques Lafitte (1767–1844), a leader of the 1830 revolution in France

384 *fiat justitia, ruat* (Latin) let justice be done, though the world perish

CONTEXT

The **epigraph** is from the poem 'The Undertaking' by John Donne (1572–1631). Donne was a Doctor of Divinity and in 1621 became Dean of St Paul's Cathedral.

CONTEXT

Henry Brougham (1778–1868) founded the Society for the Diffusion of Useful Knowledge in 1826 (see p. 378). It published relatively inexpensive pamphlets on a range of subjects, including scientific topics, to help literate members of the public to expand their education at home.

within the **narrative**. It is also a reminder that stories of individual lives are inextricably linked to broader narratives of social life and historical change.

CHAPTER 39

- Chettam persuades Dorothea to advise her uncle that he should employ Caleb Garth as farm manager.
- Brooke has a salutary encounter with one of his tenants.

Chettam summons Dorothea to Freshitt Hall to tend to Celia, who is unwell. He voices his discontent with Brooke's situation. Dorothea then visits her uncle and conveys excitedly Chettam's hope that Brooke will employ Garth and improve his farm management.

Ladislaw tells Dorothea that he has been banned from visiting the Casaubon home. She is 'anew smitten with hopelessness that she could influence Mr Casaubon's action' (p. 390).

Dorothea's carriage then takes her home. Her uncle accompanies her as far as a house occupied by Dagley, father of a boy who has been caught poaching. Brooke looks at the house in the light of his guilty conscience. Dagley has been drinking at market, and shows no respect for the landowner. He points out that Brooke does not fulfil in practice his promises in the radical press.

COMMENTARY

This chapter prefigures the failure of Brooke's political ambitions. In this respect, his aspirations resemble those of Casaubon and Lydgate, whose research projects are ultimately fruitless. The scholar and the doctor both neglect their wives, and are insensitive to their needs. As Chettam suggested in the preceding chapter, and as Dagley makes clear here, Brooke's negligence has caused real problems for his tenants, while he blindly pursues a grand reforming goal. In each case, obsession with general principles has precluded recognition of specific problems. Dorothea argues that 'we have no right to come forward and urge wider changes for good until we have tried to alter the evils which lie under our own hands' (p. 389).

CHAPTER 40

- Garth receives an invitation from Chettam to manage his estate.
- Garth tells Farebrother that Mary refused to burn Featherstone's last will.
- Farebrother invites Mary to visit his mother.

The Garth family are having breakfast. Mary, who is clearly loved by the younger children, is sewing a handkerchief for Rosamond Vincy's wedding. She has been offered and has decided to accept a teaching post in York. But Chettam has invited Caleb Garth to manage his estate, and has indicated that Brooke would like him to resume work at Tipton. To general celebration, Garth instructs Mary to decline the job in York, and stay at home with her family.

In the evening, Farebrother arrives. Fred Vincy has taken the clergyman into his confidence. Garth declares that, as he now has lucrative employment, Fred's debt no longer matters. Less magnanimously, Mary says that she will think well of Fred only when he gives her good cause. Once Mary has left the room, Garth confides to Farebrother that Featherstone had requested his daughter to burn one of the wills he had made. He adds, 'if Mary had done what he wanted, Fred Vincy would have had ten thousand pounds' (p. 406). Susan Garth vigorously defends her daughter's actions.

On his way home, Farebrother encounters Mary with her little sister Letty. He invites Mary to visit his mother, who will enjoy her

QUESTION

Mary admires Farebrother, and he is clearly attracted to her. She eventually marries Fred Vincy, but an alternative does exist for her. It is one which readers might consider preferable. Do you find the marital choices made by George Eliot's characters credible? What do they tell us about the nature of love?

company. He is attracted to Mary, and considers her too fine for the feckless Fred Vincy, but he suppresses his feelings.

Garth suggests to his wife that he should employ Fred Vincy to assist in managing the estate. She points out that Fred's parents would strongly disapprove. Garth reveals that Rigg and Bulstrode have both approached him to assess the value of Stone Court.

COMMENTARY

The **narrator** begins this chapter with talk of 'watching effects', along the lines of a scientific experiment. This reflects George Eliot's profound interest in science, but the real issue here is point of view: 'it is often necessary to change our place and examine a particular mixture or group at some distance from the point where the movement we are interested in was set up' (p. 399). A single viewpoint is not adequate to make an accurate reading of human behaviour.

CHAPTER 41

- John Raffles visits Rigg at Stone Court. Before leaving, he uses a folded piece of paper to secure his brandy flask.

Joshua Rigg is visited at Stone Court by John Raffles, his stepfather. Raffles seeks financial assistance for Rigg's mother, but Rigg, resentful of the maltreatment he and his mother have received from this man, knows that Raffles will spend any money that is offered. His mother will receive a weekly allowance, and no more.

Raffles says he will leave if Rigg gives him some brandy and a sovereign for the journey. Raffles uses a folded piece of paper to secure his brandy flask within its leather case. He then takes the stage coach to Brassing, where he joins the new railway.

COMMENTARY

The narrator tells us that the folded paper picked up and used by
Raffles to secure his flask is actually a letter from Nicholas
Bulstrode. When he later discovers this Raffles becomes aware of
Bulstrode's proposal to purchase Stone Court and he hatches a plan
to extort money from the banker. At this stage the narrator tells us
just enough to whet our appetite for another twist in the story. A
contrivance such as a piece of discarded paper picked up without
thought yet with major unforeseen consequences may appear to be
a **melodramatic** device, but it can also be read as an illustration of
the significant role played by accident and coincidence in shaping
human affairs.

CHAPTER 42

- Casaubon, anxious about the prospects for completion of his
  work, discusses his health with Lydgate.
- He discovers that Dorothea is aware that he may die suddenly.

Concerned about his illness, Casaubon still hopes 'there might be
twenty years of achievement before him, which would justify the
thirty years of preparation' (p. 420). He fears that if he should die
leaving Dorothea independent possession of his property, she would
fall prey to some ruthless predator such as Will Ladislaw.

Returning from his honeymoon, Lydgate is asked to visit Lowick
Manor. He finds Casaubon taking his habitual stroll in the Yew-
Tree Walk, and is struck by how old he looks. Casaubon's concern
is that his work should eventually be brought to print. Lydgate
offers a diagnosis of the seriousness of Casaubon's heart condition,
and he discloses that Dorothea knows of the possibility of her
husband's sudden death. Casaubon is left 'looking into the eyes of
death' (p. 424).

CHECK THE BOOK

Kirstie Blair's *Victorian Poetry and the Culture of the Heart* (Oxford University Press, 2006) is a study of literary uses of the heart and heart disease by poets such as Elizabeth Barrett Browning, Alfred Tennyson, and Matthew Arnold. Her analysis provides a useful context for consideration of Casaubon's fatal illness.

CONTEXT

René Théophile Laennec (1781–1826) was a French physician who made significant contributions to the study of heart disease. He also invented the stethoscope (p. 423). As *Middlemarch* acknowledges, French medical research during the early nineteenth century was advanced in its thinking and practices.

Dorothea joins Casaubon after Lydgate's departure, but finds her husband coldly unresponsive to her presence. He withdraws to the library; she retreats to her room, feeling wretched. She is about to send a message to her husband, saying that she is unwell and will remain in her room, when one arrives from him, indicating that he wishes to be alone that evening, and will dine in the library.

Later, suspecting that her husband has received unwelcome news from the doctor, she waits for him to come upstairs. They meet, and he speaks to her with 'kind quiet melancholy' (p. 427). Hand in hand, they walk along the broad corridor to the bedroom.

COMMENTARY

Casaubon contemplates the prospect of imminent death, his work terminated by the failure of his own constitution. He projects his frustration and sense of failure onto the world around him and, as his energies decline, he indulges in

> a perpetual suspicious conjecture that the views entertained of him were not to his advantage – a melancholy absence of passion in his efforts at achievement, and a passionate resistance to the confession that he had achieved nothing. (p. 417)

George Eliot displays considerable psychological subtlety in her portrayal of the strained marital relationship. Casaubon's egotism is such that he feels betrayed by Dorothea, who has brought the 'unappreciative world' nearer to him (p. 418). He manifests paranoia in his perception of Ladislaw, whose return 'had brought Mr Casaubon's power of suspicious construction into exasperated activity' (p. 419). From this point, his actions are governed by such suspicion.

CHAPTER 43

- Dorothea visits Lydgate's house and finds Ladislaw alone with Rosamond.

Two days later, Dorothea visits Lydgate to discuss Casaubon's health. The doctor is not at home. Dorothea seizes the opportunity to see Rosamond, but is unsettled to find her alone with Will Ladislaw. He offers to fetch Lydgate from the hospital. Dorothea insists she will go herself. Thinking of Ladislaw with Lydgate's wife, Dorothea feels confused and sheds tears. She recovers in time to converse with Lydgate. Ladislaw feels unable to continue making music with Rosamond, and says he will return another day.

Rosamond later tells her husband that she believes Ladislaw adores Dorothea. Lydgate anticipates that Dorothea will give two hundred pounds annually to the new hospital.

COMMENTARY

The music performed by Ladislaw and Rosamond contrasts with the silence prevailing at Lowick Manor. It is clear, however, that Ladislaw is besotted with Dorothea, whom he idealistically regards as a perfect woman. The contrasting characteristics of Dorothea and Rosamond are shown distinctly here.

CHAPTER 44

- After talking with Lydgate, Dorothea tells Casaubon of her plan to support the new hospital.

Lydgate tells Dorothea that her husband is displaying symptoms of anxiety. He then alerts her to the needs of the new hospital. Bulstrode's unpopularity has led to feuds which threaten the

QUESTION

The provocative title of 'Book Five' of *Middlemarch* is 'The Dead Hand'. What is the overall impact of the various titles given to the eight books comprising this novel? Do they affect the way you interpret the **narrative**?

GLOSSARY

435 **'Lungi dal caro bene'** (Italian) 'far from the well-loved', from the opera Giulio Sabino (1781) by Giuseppe Sarti

436 **leather and prunella** cobblers wore leather aprons; parsons wore prunella gowns

436 **Racine** Jean Racine (1639–99), French dramatist

CHECK THE BOOK

When George Eliot wrote *Middlemarch* there was no Welfare State. Relief for the sick, needy, and poor often depended upon voluntary assistance from wealthy benefactors. There are numerous philanthropic figures in Victorian literature; amongst the most memorable are the Cheeryble brothers in *Nicholas Nickleby* (1838–9) by Charles Dickens.

CONTEXT

The **epigraph** is from *Pseudodoxia Epidemica* (1646) by Sir Thomas Browne (1605–82). This book tackles false beliefs, superstitions, and errors of understanding across a wide range of topics. The quotation argues that human folly exists in all ages and places and suggests that our tendency to regard past times as better than our own is misguided.

project. Dorothea grows ardent in her support. At home she tells her husband she would like to pledge an annual donation from her allowance. Casaubon distrusts his wife's motives in talking to the doctor, and suspects that she is monitoring his own precarious health.

COMMENTARY

George Eliot here uses a technique comparable to cinematic **flashback** to present events occurring during the timespan of the preceding chapter.

CHAPTER 45

- There is local opposition to the new hospital and to Lydgate.

There is opposition in Middlemarch to the new hospital and to Lydgate, who is to be its chief medical superintendent. Other medical men are unsettled by his reforming spirit; they consider him arrogant, and view his success as a threat to their livelihood.

Bulstrode has provided financial support for the hospital, but is now keen to involve other contributors, as he aims to buy Stone Court. Farebrother advises Lydgate to keep his distance from the unpopular Bulstrode, and to avoid becoming hampered by personal money matters. At home, Lydgate muses on his work while Rosamond plays the piano. Rosamond says she sometimes regrets that he is a medical man. He is intolerant of such remarks.

COMMENTARY

Mrs Dollop, in Slaughter Lane, allows us a glimpse of the lower end of the Middlemarch social spectrum. Her name is evocative of stolidness, her address is sinister, and she has a disinct air of **caricature**. In the preceding chapter, Dorothea was easily won to Lydgate's cause when he identified his enemies as pettiness and ignorance. Mrs Dollop embodies these enemies. There is clearly a substantial body of prejudice against Lydgate and his innovations.

GLOSSARY

452	*vis medicatrix* (Latin) healing power
454	St John Long (1798–1834), notorious medical charlatan
455	Raspail François Raspail (1794–1878), doctor and political reformer
455	Vesalius Andrea Vesalius (1514–64), founder of modern anatomy
458	Galen (c. AD130–200), influential Greek physician

CHAPTER 46

- Ladislaw assumes an active role in local politics.
- Rosamond is pregnant.
- Lydgate is troubled by debt.

Ladislaw has become an energetic speaker as well as a writer on political issues. He assures Brooke that popular support for Reform will soon grow. The older man lacks Ladislaw's clarity of purpose. Ladislaw's unconventional behaviour arouses local suspicion, but he is a welcome guest at the Lydgate household. Rosamond is expecting a baby. Lydgate is troubled by a bill for furniture.

COMMENTARY

Ladislaw's character is more overtly unorthodox, but his engagement with the Reform movement aligns his ardent, passionate nature with those of Dorothea and Lydgate. The narrator admits that it is Ladislaw's 'desire to be where Dorothea was' that has brought him into the sphere of practical politics, but his commitment has subsequently grown in seriousness: 'Our sense of duty must often wait for some work which shall take the place of dilettantism and make us feel that the quality of our action is not a matter of indifference' (p. 461). The unconventional young man is regularly said to resemble a Romantic poet, dreaming of some lofty,

> **CONTEXT**
>
> Edmund Burke (1729–97) (p. 460) was a philosopher and political theorist best known for his influential *Reflections on the Revolution in France* (1790). Burke's liberal conservative views rejected change dictated by abstract ideas in favour of organic social Reform in response to practical needs.

GLOSSARY

462 **energumen**
fanatic

463 **galligaskins**
breeches, or baggy
leggings

465 **Stanley** Edward
Stanley, Earl of Derby
(1799–1869), Chief
Secretary for Ireland,
and later Prime
Minister

unspecified goal, but by the end of the novel he has adapted to practical requirements sufficiently to become a Member of Parliament.

CHAPTER 47

- In order to see Dorothea, Ladislaw attends a service at Lowick Church.
- The action proves misjudged.

Following an animated conversation with Lydgate, Ladislaw is kept awake considering his situation in Middlemarch. He assures himself that he does not aspire to marry Dorothea after Casaubon's death.

The next day he goes to Lowick Church, where he sits in curate Tucker's pew. He feels uncomfortable when Dorothea merely acknowledges him with a slight bow, and feels paralysed by the sight of Casaubon. He is pained to think that his presence might have caused discomfort to Dorothea, and returns home feeling saddened.

COMMENTARY

The **narrator personifies** Inclination and Objection in order to render dramatically the inner conflict Ladislaw experiences. *Middlemarch* is a novel which pays close attention to such psychological tensions within individuals.

GLOSSARY

469 **Drayton**
Michael Drayton
(1563–1631), poet

473 **Hanover** hymn
tune by William Croft
(1678–1727)

CHAPTER 48

- Casaubon increases his wife's involvement in his work, asking that she will complete it in the event of his death. His request troubles her.
- She finds him dead in the garden.

Dorothea reflects that Ladislaw's presence in the church had been a step towards reconciliation. She is hurt by her husband's refusal to acknowledge him. In her disappointment, 'it appeared that she was to live more and more in a virtual tomb' (p. 474).

After dinner, Casaubon and Dorothea retire to the library. He gives her a notebook containing a table of contents for his great work, and asks her to annotate it according to his instruction. Since the frank interview with Lydgate, Casaubon has sought to involve his wife increasingly in the project.

Waking in the night, Dorothea finds her husband in an armchair beside the fading fire. He asks her to continue the work they began earlier, and requests Dorothea's compliance with his wishes in the event of his death. She cannot promise to observe his instructions without knowing the details. He sleeps, but his request keeps her awake. She dreads the prospect of having to sift 'those mixed heaps of material, which were to be the doubtful illustration of principles still more doubtful' (p. 478).

Next morning, Tantripp, the maid, notices Dorothea's paleness. As Dorothea enters the library, Casaubon is preparing to walk in the garden. He asks for an answer to his request, made the night before, and she promises to join him shortly in the Yew-Tree Walk. She feels trapped by 'the ideal and not the real yoke of marriage' (p. 481). Then she discovers her husband's dead body. Later, as Lydgate attends her, she is tormented by her failure to comply with Casaubon's request.

CONTEXT

The actual nature of Casaubon's research is comparative mythology – the search for shared themes and characteristics in myths from different cultures. It has been a thriving discipline during the years since *Middlemarch* was first published. Linguistic, structural and psychological approaches have proven especially fruitful. Casaubon's work, nonetheless, seems to be a dusty obsession, out of touch with the living world.

COMMENTARY

Casaubon's death is preceded by noticeable diminution of his energy. This decline is thrown into sharp relief by the fact that Celia has recently had a baby. Her contented and fruitful marriage contrasts with the sterility of Dorothea's 'spiritual emptiness and discontent' (p. 475). Moreover, Dorothea recognises that Casaubon's work is governed by 'a theory which was already withered in the birth like an elfin child' (p. 478). Casaubon's work now appears to Dorothea as 'a mosaic wrought from crushed ruins' (p. 478).

GLOSSARY

474 **Keble's Christian Year** popular collection of poems, published in 1827, by John Keble

478 **Lavoisier** Antoine Lavoisier (1743–94), pioneer of modern chemistry

479 **Gog and Magog** nations led by Satan in the battle of Armageddon (Revelation 20:8)

CHAPTER 49

- Chettam is appalled by a codicil added to Casaubon's will.
- Speaking with Brooke, he insists that Ladislaw should be sent away from the area.

On the day following Casaubon's burial, while Dorothea is confined to her bed still in a state of shock, Chettam speaks with Brooke. Casaubon has added a codicil which Chettam recognises as 'a positive insult to Dorothea' (p. 484). Chettam insists that Ladislaw must be sent away from the area, and that Dorothea should stay with Celia and the baby. Chettam is clearly concerned that people will suppose Dorothea gave Casaubon some reason to feel jealous of Ladislaw as a rival for her affections. Brooke, however, is keen to retain Ladislaw's services.

COMMENTARY

George Eliot patterns vocabulary carefully, in order to clarify relationships between characters. In recent chapters, both Casaubon and Dorothea have been described as 'melancholy', indicating the state of their marriage in its last stages. Similarly, the word 'disgust' was used to register the response of Chettam, Celia, and Ladislaw upon learning of Dorothea's engagement to Casaubon.

George Eliot may consciously have been making a pun on the word 'will' here. The codicil to Casaubon's will is a mean-spirited attempt to frustrate Will Ladislaw. Featherstone's will also results in frustrated hopes. But throughout *Middlemarch* the efforts of living characters to exercise the power of their will run into serious obstacles.

CHAPTER 50

- Dorothea learns of the codicil prohibiting her marriage to Ladislaw while she remains owner of Lowick Manor.
- She attends to her husband's papers.
- Lydgate recommends the appointment of Farebrother as rector of Lowick.

Dorothea stays at Freshitt Hall, but she wishes to examine her husband's papers, and is keen to determine who should succeed him as rector of Lowick. Brooke insists there is no urgency.

After their uncle's departure, Celia reveals that Casaubon's will has decreed that Dorothea should lose Lowick Manor if she were to marry Ladislaw. Celia feels confident that her sister would never consider marrying Ladislaw, but Dorothea is in turmoil. She experiences 'a sudden strange yearning of heart towards Will Ladislaw' (p. 490).

Dorothea determines to go to Lowick in order to start to put things in order. She has the support of Lydgate, who tells Chettam: 'She wants perfect freedom, I think, more than any other prescription' (p. 491). Next day, Chettam drives her to Lowick Manor. She attends to her husband's papers, finding no intimate message, but instead a Synoptical Tabulation setting out the structure of his work.

CHECK THE BOOK

Clergymen performed a prominent social role in nineteenth-century England and consequently they often feature in Victorian literature. See, for example, Anthony Trollope's *Barchester Towers* (1857), or George Eliot's own *Scenes of Clerical Life* (1857).

GLOSSARY

494 **Latimer** Hugh Latimer (1485–1555), archbishop famed for his sermons

496 **Daphnis** in Greek mythology, the son of Hermes, taught by Pan to play the flute

Lydgate recommends Farebrother as a suitable successor to the living of Lowick, praising his 'plain, easy eloquence' (p. 494), while not concealing his weakness for card-playing and gambling. Dorothea longs for a display of 'primitive zeal' (p. 495), and initially favours Tyke. But she is drawn to the possibility of saving Farebrother from his weakness by materially improving his lot. Lydgate affirms that Ladislaw would also sing Farebrother's praises.

COMMENTARY

The choice between Tyke and Farebrother to become rector recalls the earlier contest for the hospital chaplaincy. It is an opportunity for Lydgate to compensate for his earlier failure to support Farebrother, despite his friendship with him.

Dorothea dresses as a widow. Her sombre appearance contrasts with the lavender and white dress worn by Celia. Beneath the sobriety, however, Dorothea's emotional life is revitalised by her understanding that others are capable of seeing Ladislaw as a potential suitor for her. Unlike Casaubon, who withdrew from the web of social relationships, Ladislaw is a significant, if unsettling, presence in the lives of others: 'he was a creature who entered into every one's feelings, and could take the pressure of their thought instead of urging his own with iron resistance' (p. 496).

CHAPTER 51

- Brooke's political ambitions end in chaos.

Ladislaw is not aware of the codicil, but recognises that his reputation will suffer from proximity to the recently widowed young woman. He is preoccupied with preparation for the imminent election, although Brooke has started to dissuade Ladislaw from regular attendance at Tipton Grange.

Brooke makes a chaotic electoral address from the balcony of the White Hart inn. An effigy of him appears in the crowd. His voice is mimicked and eggs are thrown. The speech draws to a premature halt. Soon afterwards, Brooke resigns his candidacy. He decides to give up the *Pioneer*, and suggests that Ladislaw should find other employment. But Ladislaw is determined not to leave the area until it suits him.

COMMENTARY

Brooke refers to Ladislaw as 'a sort of Burke with a leaven of Shelley' (p. 499). These **analogies** may recall Dorothea's earlier perception of Casaubon as comparable to Locke and Milton. In each case **allusion** to representative famous men is intended to elucidate the character of their local equivalent, but often it is a distorted appraisal that results.

CHECK THE BOOK

Felix Holt, the Radical (1866), the novel by George Eliot that preceded *Middlemarch*, is centrally concerned with an election held in a small town in the English Midlands at the time of the First Reform Act in 1832.

CONTEXT

Percy Bysshe Shelley (1792–1822), son of a Sussex landowner, was a major **Romantic** poet who conducted his life in a spirit of unswerving idealism. That idealism is here contrasted with Edmund Burke's practical approach to political issues (see Chapter 46). Shelley responded to social injustice through rousing radical poems such as 'The Mask of Anarchy' and 'To the Men of England'.

GLOSSARY	
498	**plumpers** those who vote for only one candidate, when they might vote for more
499	**ten-pound householders** entitlement to vote was granted in the Reform Act to occupants of property valued at ten pounds or more
503	**Pope** Alexander Pope (1688–1744), poet
504	**Johnson** Samuel Johnson (1709–84), poet, lexicographer, and critic
505	**Chatham** William Pitt, Earl of Chatham (1708–78), Whig statesman
505	**Pitt** William Pitt the Younger (1759–1806), second son of Chatham, twice Prime Minister
507	**'eating his dinners'** studying law
508	**Althorpe** John Charles Spencer, Viscount Althorpe (1782–1845), Chancellor of the Exchequer, 1830–4

CHAPTER 52

- Farebrother is appointed rector of Lowick.
- Fred Vincy completes his degree, and asks Farebrother to recommend him to Mary Garth.

In June, to his family's delight, Farebrother learns that he is to be rector of Lowick. A week later he receives a visit from Fred Vincy, who has completed his degree. Fred asks Farebrother to speak with Mary Garth, on his behalf, concerning the possibility of marriage if he were to become a clergyman.

Farebrother visits Mary and argues the case for Fred. She considers Fred entirely unsuited to be a clergyman, and declares 'I could not love a man who is ridiculous' (p. 516).

Farebrother mentions that he knows from her father of Mary's uneasiness concerning her refusal to burn Featherstone's second will. He assures her that the first will would not have withstood a legal challenge if the second had been burnt.

Mary senses Farebrother's love for her. Still, she declares she could never be happy knowing that Fred was unhappy on account of losing her. Her eyes fill with tears upon recognition of Farebrother's selfless generosity.

COMMENTARY

We share Mary's recognition that Farebrother loves her, and it is tempting to consider him a more appropriate husband for her than Fred Vincy. Unlike Dorothea, however, she is not blinkered by her admiration for an older man, and although she respects Farebrother, her long standing friendship with Fred will later prove a substantial basis for marriage, once he has found an appropriate direction in life.

CHAPTER 53

- Bulstrode buys Stone Court.
- Raffles arrives, and seeks to extort money from the banker.

Bulstrode buys Stone Court from Rigg, but does not intend to live there until his business commitments have lessened. Rigg leaves to become a money-changer in a busy port. His contented materialism contrasts starkly with the insatiable idealism which drives Dorothea, Lydgate, and Ladislaw.

One evening, Bulstrode is talking with Caleb Garth when John Raffles arrives. Raffles has been drinking, and speaks to Bulstrode with crude familiarity. He has come with news that Rigg's mother has died, but Raffles is pleased to renew acquaintance with 'Nick' Bulstrode. He has now read the paper he used to secure his flask on his visit to Rigg and alludes to it as 'what you may call a providential thing' (p. 522).

Raffles refers to shameful circumstances surrounding Bulstrode's first marriage, and reveals his intention to extort money from the banker. Bulstrode gives Raffles food and drink and invites him to stay overnight. He returns to talk with him the following morning. Bulstrode is willing to pay Raffles to stay away. Raffles refuses to surrender his liberty for an annuity. Bulstrode feels 'abjectly in the power of this loud invulnerable man' (p. 529).

Raffles mentions that he has traced Sarah, the estranged daughter of Bulstrode's wealthy first wife, and has discovered the name of her husband: 'It began with L; it was almost all l's, I fancy' (p. 530). The name was, in fact, Ladislaw. That afternoon Raffles departs. Bulstrode dreads the prospect of his return.

COMMENTARY

Raffles is an incarnation of the past for Bulstrode. This is one of numerous instances in *Middlemarch* where the past's dead hand is seen to clutch the living present. Bulstrode's first marriage to an old

The **epigraph** translates as 'Love resides in the eyes of my Lady; for they grant nobility to everything she beholds. Wherever she goes, men turn and stare, and if she greets someone his heart flutters, his downcast face grows pale and he sighs at his own unworthiness: hatred turns into love and pride becomes an admirer. Ladies, please help to honour her. Humility and benevolence are brought into the mind by her words, and whoever beholds her is granted many blessings. When she gives a little smile her look eludes words and cannot be held in the mind; it is such a new and noble miracle.' The quotation is from Dante Alighieri's (*c.* 1265–1321) discourse on love, *La Vita Nuova* (The New Life) (1295).

and wealthy woman inverts the terms of Dorothea's marriage to Casaubon with regard to relative ages of husband and wife and to motivation.

Chapter 54

- Dorothea returns to live alone at Lowick Manor.
- Ladislaw calls to tell her of his imminent departure for London.

Dorothea returns to Lowick Manor after three months at Freshitt Hall. Her uncle has gone abroad following the election debacle, and her friends express concern at Dorothea living alone. Mrs Cadwallader is keen that Dorothea should marry again but, aware of the codicil, she advocates intervention, fearing 'a worse business than the Casaubon business yet' (p. 538).

Dorothea feels a helpless longing to meet Ladislaw. One morning, she is attending to paperwork when he is announced. Their meeting is emotionally charged yet necessarily restrained. He intends to go to London and become a barrister, as a preliminary for public life. The arrival of Chettam hastens Ladislaw's departure.

Commentary

George Eliot repeatedly indicates in this novel that human beings do not exist in isolation but are caught up in a web of social relationships. Dorothea lives alone at this point but the care of others and her own desires connect her with the world beyond the walls of Lowick Manor.

CHAPTER 55

- Prospects for a second marriage are discussed by her friends, but Dorothea vows she will not marry again.

Ladislaw's departure upsets Dorothea. She is still dressed in mourning, and is not prepared to admit to herself that she has fallen in love. One warm evening at Freshitt Hall, Celia insists on removing from Dorothea the close cap she has become accustomed to wear as a widow. Mrs Cadwallader provocatively talks of errors in marriage. Later that evening, Dorothea vows to Celia that she will never marry again.

COMMENTARY

Dorothea's characteristic inclination to self-sacrifice is to the fore in this chapter; she renounces the possibility of marrying again. Her personal aspiration is more broadly social:

> I should like to take a great deal of land, and drain it, and make a little colony, where everybody should work, and all the work should be done well. I should know every one of the people and be their friend. (p. 550)

For further discussion of this idea see **Themes: Altruism and egotism**.

> **GLOSSARY**
>
> 550 **Dido** queen of Carthage, deserted by Aeneas
>
> 550 **Zenobia** queen of Palmyra, enslaved by Emperor Aurelian

CHAPTER 56

- The railway has come to Middlemarch.
- Caleb Garth and Fred Vincy protect railway agents who are physically attacked by hostile local labourers.

Dorothea employs Caleb Garth to help improve her land and build cottages. She admires his efficiency, and he is impressed by her understanding of practical matters.

> **CONTEXT**
>
> The epigraph is from a poem entitled 'The Character of a Happy Life' by writer and diplomat Sir Henry Wotton (1568–1639).

CONTEXT

Local resistance to the advent of railways may now seem foolishly conservative, but technology was altering life in rural England in fundamental ways. In 1840 the Great Western Railway company introduced a coordinated measurement of time to enable their trains to run according to a fixed schedule. Other companies soon followed suit for their region. Before adoption of this so-called 'railway time' there was significant variation in local time measurement across the countryside.

CONTEXT

Greenwich Mean Time was legally adopted as the standard measure throughout Great Britain in 1880. Railway companies had prepared the country for this important act of standardisation.

A railway line is to be run through Lowick parish. Local people view the innovation with suspicion and apprehension. Caleb Garth visits a farm on Dorothea's behalf. Fred Vincy, riding nearby, sees Garth and his assistant rushing to help four railway agents who are being attacked by farm labourers. Fred intervenes, winning the gratitude of Garth, whose assistant has been injured. Garth speaks to the labourers, hoping to change their perception of the new development.

Fred expresses a desire to become Garth's assistant, rather than entering the Church. He also expresses his love for Mary. Garth consults his wife before employing Fred. Susan Garth assents tearfully, after arguing that Fred is not good enough for Mary, especially as Farebrother is a potential suitor.

The following morning, Garth tests Fred's writing and numeracy skills. He is dismayed at the illegibility of the young gentleman's writing, which is quite unsuitable for business, and Fred is disturbed by the prospect of desk-work. Nonetheless, Garth offers to take him on.

Fred tells his parents of the arrangement, speaking first with his father, at his warehouse. Vincy shows his displeasure, but tells Fred to stick with it now he has arrived at a decision. Mrs Vincy on the other hand is inconsolable, fearing that her son will marry Mary Garth. Vincy eventually reconciles his wife to the situation, especially as Rosamond has miscarried her baby, and Lydgate has money troubles. Vincy says he will not assist Lydgate, as he never really approved of the marriage.

COMMENTARY

In this chapter we see characters grappling with difficult social issues and reacting to them very differently. Fred Vincy wishes to punish the labourers for their violence, but Garth recognises that its basis is pettiness and ignorance, and seeks to educate them towards acceptance of the railway. Lydgate encounters comparable resistance to his medical innovations, but instead of responding with the measured understanding shown by Garth, he chooses to ignore the opposition, and suffers the consequences. Garth, like his daughter, is a model of practical good sense. That makes his deference to his wife's view of most matters all the more striking. Such considerate accommodation of another's point of view is rare in the novel, and is distant from Dorothea's experience with Casaubon, or Rosamond's with Lydgate.

CHAPTER 57

- Discussing his own prospects with Mrs Garth, Fred Vincy learns that Farebrother is in love with Mary.

CONTEXT

The **epigraph** refers to the writings of Sir Walter Scott (1771–1832), a prolific and hugely popular Scottish historical novelist, who died around the time in which *Middlemarch* is set.

Fred Vincy visits the Garths. Christy, their studious eldest son, is home on holiday. Fred talks with Mrs Garth about his own prospects. She discloses that Farebrother is in love with Mary. Fred proceeds to Lowick Parsonage to tell Mary of Christy's arrival and of his own appointment as her father's assistant. When Farebrother arrives, Fred feels 'horribly jealous' (p. 578).

When they are alone, Fred tells Mary that he foresees her marriage to Farebrother as inevitable. Mary is surprised and annoyed. She has fleeting visions of an alternative future, but her commitment to Fred remains unshaken.

COMMENTARY

The presence of Christy reminds us that the Garths view education as an essential means of social advancement for their sons. Money given earlier to settle Fred Vincy's debts had been reserved to enable their younger son Alfred to train as an engineer. Mary, on the other hand, is offered no such educational opportunity. Her mother, for all her sympathetic kindness, is convinced that women should remain subordinate to men. Her ambition is that Mary should marry well, and Farebrother is her preference (see **Themes: The role of women**).

GLOSSARY

571 **Porson** Richard Porson (1759–1808), classical scholar

CONTEXT

The **epigraph** is taken from Shakespeare's 'Sonnet 93'.

CHAPTER 58

- Lydgate's debts increase. His and Rosamond's furniture must be inventoried as security against debts.
- Their marriage is put under increasing strain.

CONTEXT

In this chapter, Ladislaw attends a meeting to discuss a Mechanics' Institute (p. 592). Such Institutes were established to provide libraries, lecture courses, and technical training for the benefit of working men. They were often funded by local industrialists who recognised the advantages to be gained from a skilled work force. The first Mechanics' Institute was established in Glasgow in 1823; others followed in London and Manchester in 1824, and then in numerous towns throughout Britain.

Evident tensions have developed within the marriage between Lydgate and Rosamond. They find a focus in Captain Lydgate, a cousin of Lydgate's. During his visit the Captain impresses Rosamond; her husband finds him ill-mannered. As a consequence of a minor accident while horse-riding with Captain Lydgate, Rosamond gives birth prematurely to a still-born baby.

Returning home one evening Lydgate finds Ladislaw making music with Rosamond and cannot conceal his ill-humour. Ladislaw tactfully departs.

Lydgate reveals to Rosamond the extent of his debts. He has to give security, and an inventory, or list, of their furniture must be made. He insists this is a temporary measure and demands that Rosamond should not tell her father. She sobs, and suggests they move from Middlemarch to London, or closer to Lydgate's family, who live near Durham.

The couple become temporarily estranged: 'It seemed that she had no more identified herself with him than if they had been creatures of different species and opposing interests' (p. 597). A degree of accord is restored, but Lydgate anticipates with dread 'the necessity for a complete change in their way of living' (p. 598).

COMMENTARY

Captain Lydgate features marginally in the novel, but reference to him in this chapter does highlight the radically different points of view from which Lydgate and Rosamond look at the world. Lydgate pursues a vision of the contribution to the wider world he can make through his medical work. Rosamond's concerns are more immediate and grounded in material prosperity and social status.

The divergence in their understanding results in the increasing instability of their marriage.

Rosamond's complete lack of respect for her husband's learning stands in stark contrast to Dorothea's initial reverence for Casaubon: 'His superior knowledge and mental force, instead of being, as he had imagined, a shrine to consult on all occasions, was simply set aside on every practical question' (p. 586). Just as Dorothea came to realise that Casaubon was not the husband for whom she had hoped, so Lydgate is no longer able to perceive his wife as a 'perfect piece of womanhood' (p. 583). Ladislaw, who is sensitive to others, is said to have 'more comprehension of Lydgate than Rosamond had' (p. 592). Similarly, he manifests understanding of Dorothea which her husband lacked.

CHAPTER 59

- Ladislaw learns of Casaubon's codicil from Rosamond and is appalled.

At Lowick Parsonage, Fred Vincy hears of Casaubon's codicil from the assembled group of ladies. He mentions it to Rosamond, who relays the news to her husband. Lydgate instructs her not to tell Ladislaw, but she ignores him and reveals the secret. Ladislaw is appalled at his cousin's 'foul insult' (p. 601). Rosamond feels vaguely jealous of Dorothea. She is further disgruntled because, against her husband's express wishes, she has sought assistance from her father, and has been rebuffed.

COMMENTARY

Rosamond grows increasingly defiant of her husband's instructions. She attempts to act independently, but each move creates a further tangle in the web of social relationships.

CHECK THE BOOK
Gilbert White (1720–93), was a clergyman and author of *The Natural History of Selborne* (1788–9) (Penguin Books, 1977), a charming account of his meticulous observations of wildlife in a Hampshire parish which has remained in print continuously since its publication. The intense sense of local knowledge based in keen observation that White conveys is in stark contrast to the kind of abstract and disembodied understanding represented by Casaubon in *Middlemarch*.

CHAPTER 60

CONTEXT

The **epigraph** is from Act III Scene 2 of Shakespeare's *King Henry IV, Part Two*, in which Justice Shallow is an aptly named officer of the law.

• Ladislaw is confronted by Raffles, who knew his parents.

A few days later, Borthrop Trumbull oversees an auction of articles from a furnished mansion recently purchased by Mr Larcher, the carrier. Bulstrode has asked Ladislaw to attend in order to give his expert opinion on a picture which Mrs Bulstrode wishes to buy. After securing purchase of the picture, Ladislaw is confronted by Raffles, who asks if his mother was called Sarah Dunkirk. Ladislaw says she was, but his aggressive attitude deters Raffles from further conversation.

Later that evening, however, Raffles overtakes Ladislaw in the street and renews the conversation. This time he talks of Will's father, whom he met in Boulogne. He refers to Will's mother running away from her own mother and the world of 'respectable thieving' in which she was raised (p. 611), to pursue a career on the stage. Ladislaw is disturbed by a sense that this unsavoury man has revealed details of her life which his mother withheld from him.

COMMENTARY

Trumbull, with his verbal pedantry, introduces a comic element which momentarily lightens the novel's tone.

For Ladislaw, as for Bulstrode, Raffles is an embodiment of the past, giving voice to long suppressed secrets, and altering their sense of the present. The pawnbroking business run by Ladislaw's grandmother is said to have knowingly received stolen goods. This reveals a vulgar side to the march of the middle classes, as commercial enterprise veers into criminality.

GLOSSARY	
602	**Gibbons** Grinling Gibbons (1648–1721), famous wood-carver
603	**Guido** probably Guido Reni (1575–1642), Italian painter

604	'Berghems' Nicholas Berghem (1620–83), Dutch painter
607	Slender foolish young man in Shakespeare's *The Merry Wives of Windsor*
609	'Full many a gem', as the poet says reference to Thomas Gray's 'Elegy Written in a Country Churchyard' (1751)

CHAPTER 61

- Raffles speaks with Mrs Bulstrode. Bulstrode ponders his involvement with the Dunkirk family, and his first marriage to Ladislaw's grandmother.
- He discloses that relationship to Ladislaw, and offers him compensatory payment.
- Ladislaw disdainfully rejects the offer.

CONTEXT

The epigraph is from *The History of Rasselas, Prince of Abissinia*, a short novel by Samuel Johnson (1709–84). It is set in exotic locations but shares with *Middlemarch* a thematic concern with how the choices we make shape the course of our lives.

The same night, Bulstrode returns home from business to discover that Raffles has spoken with his wife, who has only fragmentary knowledge of her husband's past, and of his first marriage. The following evening, Mrs Bulstrode notices that her husband looks unwell.

Bulstrode muses on his past, his friendship with the Dunkirk family, and employment within their business as pawnbrokers. Mrs Dunkirk's husband and son died, and her daughter ran away. The widow grew attached to Bulstrode. Eventually they married, and he became, on her death five years after the marriage, sole inheritor of her wealth. However, he and Raffles knew that the daughter had actually been found: a circumstance which might have precluded the marriage. The inheritance would then have passed to Mrs Dunkirk's grandson, Will Ladislaw. The business collapsed after a further thirteen years, by which time Bulstrode had consolidated his position as banker, churchman, and public benefactor.

Bulstrode invites Ladislaw to meet him at his home, The Shrubs, that evening, when his wife and daughters are out. Ladislaw is struck by the banker's sickly appearance. Bulstrode discloses the ties which connect them, including his enrichment through marriage to Ladislaw's grandmother. Ladislaw feels a mixture of pity and contempt, and is disturbed by the revelation that his family has been engaged in an occupation which he considers dishonourable. His mother reacted against the stain on the family's honour, and he intends to follow her course. The repentant Bulstrode is not allowed the satisfaction of a compensatory gesture. After Ladislaw's departure Bulstrode weeps 'like a woman' (p. 624), although he recovers his composure before his wife and daughters return. His sole consolation is that Ladislaw will not broadcast the evening's revelations.

QUESTION

Is George Eliot simply conforming to a gender stereotype when she writes that Bulstrode weeps 'like a woman'?

COMMENTARY

The complexity of that web of social relationships which creates the fabric of Middlemarch life is vividly rendered through the disclosure that Bulstrode married Ladislaw's maternal grandmother, and consequently deprived him of a substantial inheritance. The revelation may recall the surprise appearance of Joshua Rigg at Featherstone's funeral, dashing Fred Vincy's hope of a legacy. In both cases we see the surfacing of connections long suppressed in the name of middle class respectability.

Bulstrode's particular situation is translated into a general psychological observation: 'The terror of being judged sharpens the memory: it sends an inevitable glare over the long-unvisited past which has been habitually recalled only in general phrases'. The **narrator** describes a man's past as 'a still quivering part of himself' (p. 615). The **epic** scope of *Middlemarch* enables George Eliot to encompass such insights into interior states as well as offering a coherent portrait of English provincial life in the early 1830s.

CHAPTER 62

- Dorothea is upset by Mrs Cadwallader's adverse remarks concerning Ladislaw and Rosamond.
- She returns home to find Ladislaw waiting for her. He announces his imminent departure from Middlemarch.

Next morning, Ladislaw determines to leave Middlemarch as soon as possible. He writes to Dorothea asking to see her once more before his departure.

Dorothea is visiting her sister at Freshitt Hall. At Chettam's contrivance, Mrs Cadwallader broaches the subject of Dorothea's relationship with Ladislaw. She comments on the impropriety of his regular visits to Rosamond's house. Dorothea protests at this misrepresentation of his behaviour. Mrs Cadwallader laments Lydgate's unsuitable marriage. Dorothea departs haughtily before anything further can be said. During the journey back to Tipton Grange she weeps.

Dorothea finds Ladislaw waiting in her library. He speaks of the insult he has suffered through Casaubon's will. She assures him that she never doubted his integrity. Their feelings cannot be expressed openly, and neither is sure how the other really feels. Dorothea initially suspects that he loves Rosamond, with whom he has spent more time alone, but after his departure she is filled with the conviction that she is herself the woman that Ladislaw loves.

Driving to Lowick Manor she overtakes Ladislaw walking, and he raises his hat. He remains unsure whether she loves him. After spending the evening with the Lydgates, he departs the following day.

COMMENTARY

Mrs Cadwallader's lamentation over Lydgate's unsuitable marriage corresponds to her reaction to Dorothea's marriage, and forms another small link between the experiences of those two characters.

CONTEXT

The **epigraph** is from *The Squire of Low Degree*, a verse romance written by an unknown author during the late fifteenth century. It is about a poor young man who seeks to marry a king's daughter.

www. CHECK THE NET

The word 'weepers' (p. 635) refers to black crape veils worn by widows. During the nineteenth century mourning for the dead was generally observed with great formality and gravity. When Queen Victoria's husband Prince Albert died in 1861, she went into a prolonged phase of deep mourning. A sense of the etiquette of formal mourning in 1886 can be obtained from the American fashion magazine article at **www. victoriana.com**. Click on 'Search' and enter 'funeral' into the search box.

CHAPTER 63

• Farebrother learns of Lydgate's financial problems.

At a Christmas dinner party, Farebrother discusses Lydgate's work for the new hospital and is told that Lydgate has financial problems. There is speculation that he may receive support from his wealthy relatives.

At a New Year's Day party hosted by Vincy, Farebrother tells Lydgate that he will lend a friendly ear when needed. Lydgate, who has helped advance Farebrother's situation, is nonetheless mortified by the offer of help. He feels his private life has been exposed to public view.

Mary Garth's popularity with Mrs Vincy's youngest daughters softens their mother's view of her. Farebrother's relatives still hope he may marry Mary.

COMMENTARY

The contrast between altruism and egotism is a major theme of *Middlemarch*. Some characters (such as Bulstrode) are governed in their actions by self-interest. Others (such as Dorothea) are driven by desire to assist others. Farebrother is an altruistic man, but helping others depends upon their receptivity, and Lydgate bridles at Farebrother's offer of support (see **Themes: Altruism and egotism**).

CHAPTER 64

• As his debts deepen, Lydgate decides to lease his house.
• Rosamond takes steps to ensure this does not happen, and writes to Lydgate's uncle, asking for money.

Lydgate requires a thousand pounds to clear his debts. His mood deteriorates and his relationship with Rosamond grows increasingly troubled as their financial situation worsens. He suggests that they find cheaper accommodation, and also that Ned Plymdale (Rosamond's former suitor), who is to marry Sophy Toller, might be interested in their house and furniture. Rosamond is reduced to tears, and filled with resentment. In silence she leaves the room, resolved to hinder her husband's plans. She visits Ned Plymdale's mother and denies she knows anything about their house being available, then Trumbull's office, where she countermands her husband's instruction to lease their property.

That evening, she tells Lydgate that she has visited Ned Plymdale's mother and has ascertained that he has found another house: another untruth. He discloses the current extent of his debts. The next day Rosamond writes to Lydgate's uncle, Sir Godwin, asking for money. By New Year's Day no reply has arrived. Rosamond confesses that she has cancelled her husband's instructions to Trumbull. Lydgate is thrown into inner turmoil as his wife chastises him for not attaining the social position she had anticipated when they married. Lydgate, unaware of his wife's letter to Sir Godwin, considers with distaste the prospect of a visit to his uncle to ask for financial assistance.

QUESTION

In the preceding chapter we saw the strength of Lydgate's self-esteem. Do you view it as inexcusable pride, or an acceptable concern for personal honour?

COMMENTARY

This sequence of events precedes the party at which Farebrother sought to console Lydgate. This is another example of the technique, comparable to cinematic **flashback**, which George Eliot uses to supply a different angle on events.

In this chapter, Rosamond's self-esteem drives her to contradict her husband's instructions. There is vanity in her response, but that failing is surely made worse by Lydgate's habit of treating her as a child. Their marriage resulted from selfish concerns: Lydgate saw Rosamond as a decorative enhancement; she saw him as a means to social elevation. In effect, they now inhabit separate worlds.

George Eliot shows that Rosamond's dependent femininity, which is largely a product of her education, prevents her attaining sympathetic understanding of Lydgate's precarious position (see **Themes: The role of women**). The doctor shows no understanding of the reasons underlying 'her negative character – her want of sensibility, which showed itself in disregard both of his specific wishes and of his general aims' (p. 652). Rosamond, on the other hand, cannot comprehend that 'the Lydgate she had been in love with had been a group of airy conditions for her, most of which had disappeared' (p. 661). Mary Garth's compassionate and practical response to Fred Vincy's money troubles provides an obvious contrast.

CHAPTER 65

CONTEXT

The **epigraph** is from the Wife of Bath's 'Prologue' in the *Canterbury Tales* by Geoffrey Chaucer (c. 1343–1400).

- A condescending letter arrives from Lydgate's uncle.

Lydgate intends to visit his uncle at Quallingham, but keeps the plan from Rosamond. Then, a letter arrives from Sir Godwin. Rosamond excitedly presents the letter to her husband. He is furious. The letter is contemptuous of a man who gets his wife to beg on his behalf. Sir Godwin declares he cannot make any useful connections for his nephew, asserting 'I have nothing to do with men of your profession' (p. 664).

Rosamond cries at Lydgate's angry words. He criticises her secrecy and deviousness. She confronts him with failure to provide for her in an appropriate fashion. She says he has exposed her to ridicule, and proclaims dramatically: 'I wish I had died with the baby' (p. 667). He embraces her as she weeps, but he is unable to say anything.

COMMENTARY

Many social relationships in *Middlemarch* are presented as the exercise of power by one individual over another. For example,

Featherstone derives obvious pleasure from the control he wields over Fred Vincy and Mary Garth. Lydgate shows a glimmer of sympathetic understanding when he recognises that Rosamond has no such distraction from wretchedness as his own work provides for him. But the limits to his understanding are telling: 'it was inevitable that in that excusing mood he should think of her as if she were an animal of another feebler species. Nevertheless she had mastered him' (p. 667). The concluding sentence casts the patriarchal figure as the loser in a struggle. He seems incapable of conceiving marriage as a state of mutual respect.

CHAPTER 66

- Lydgate plays billiards in a desperate attempt to win money.
- Farebrother exhorts Fred Vincy to act in a manner deserving of Mary Garth's love.

Lydgate grows increasingly desperate. One evening, he visits the Green Dragon inn hoping to purchase a cheaper horse. He plays billiards and starts to win money. Fred Vincy arrives, and is astonished to find his brother-in-law behaving so uncharacteristically. Farebrother arrives just as the doctor has started to lose money. Lydgate greets him politely, then leaves. The rector asks Fred to accompany him to St Botolph's church. Farebrother speaks of his own affection for Mary, and exhorts Fred to conduct himself in a manner worthy of her affection.

COMMENTARY

The **narrator** has earlier referred to character as 'a process and an unfolding' (p. 149). Lydgate's uncharacteristic behaviour is a good illustration of the way circumstances may determine the nature of that process and unfolding (see **Characterisation**).

CHECK THE BOOK

Rosamond miscarries her baby despite being married to a doctor. In the early nineteenth century the experience of miscarriage and the deaths of mothers during childbirth were far more common than they are today. Rosamond's declaration, 'I wish I had died with the baby', would have been resonant for George Eliot's contemporaries. Such maternal deaths in childbirth feature in Charles Dickens's *Dombey and Son* (1846–8) and in Emily Brontë's *Wuthering Heights* (1848).

CONTEXT

The epigraph is spoken by Lord Angelo in Shakespeare's *Measure for Measure*, Act II Scene 1 (1604).

CHECK THE BOOK

Middlemarch is a novel that starts with reference to a saint, but it is set in a material world where the need for money is a major concern. Lydgate, in his desperation resorts to gambling. Gambling with cards features prominently in Charles Dickens's *The Old Curiosity Shop* (1841) (Penguin Books, 2001) and gambling at the race track is a key element in Anthony Trollope's *The Duke's Children* (1880) (Penguin Books, 2006).

CHAPTER 67

- Bulstrode is taken ill, and Lydgate advises him to rest.
- The doctor alludes to his own money troubles, but Bulstrode offers no help.

Next morning, Lydgate feels ashamed that he has added to his debt. He now views Rosamond's suggestion that they should leave Middlemarch as a distasteful possibility. Despondently, he considers approaching Bulstrode for assistance. He has noted a deterioration in Bulstrode's health, and a corresponding reduction in the energy he can invest in the hospital.

Called to attend to Bulstrode at the bank, Lydgate diagnoses stress, and advocates that he takes a rest from business. Bulstrode declares his intention to spend time by the coast. He will withdraw support from the hospital.

Lydgate discloses his own financial difficulties. Bulstrode, who feels he has given enough support to Vincy's family, suggests unsympathetically that the doctor should declare himself bankrupt.

COMMENTARY

In seeking help from Bulstrode, Lydgate is again acting in an uncharacteristic manner. His hopes are dashed not because Bulstrode feels animosity towards him, but because the banker perceives him in the context of Vincy's family. This is further evidence that however much individual characters may aspire to live independently, they are inextricably caught up in a web of social relationships.

CHAPTER 68

- Raffles continues his extortion of money from Bulstrode.
- Bulstrode invites Caleb Garth to manage Stone Court.

This chapter takes us back to Christmas Eve. Raffles reappears at The Shrubs. Bulstrode considers it prudent to keep him there, rather than sending him into town. But the drunken Raffles proves 'hopelessly unmanageable' (p. 686). Bulstrode grows defiant, and early on Christmas Day he escorts the unwelcome guest from his premises, giving him one hundred pounds with promise of more if he stays away.

Bulstrode asks Caleb Garth to manage Stone Court. Garth advises him to let the property and take part of the proceeds annually. Bulstrode agrees to a proposal that Fred Vincy should manage the farm under Garth's supervision.

COMMENTARY

As the various strands of the novel develop, chronological disruptions in the storyline and leaps back in time supply information we need in order to make sense of events.

Bulstrode likes to be in control, and to manipulate others. He gives money to Raffles believing it will hasten his self-destruction through drinking and dissolute living. In this belief he is proved correct, but before long it becomes apparent that control of an individual is not enough to ensure control of events, which have unforeseen ramifications.

CHAPTER 69

- Garth encounters Raffles, who is unwell, and takes him to Stone Court. He informs Bulstrode, who summons Lydgate to assist.
- Garth says he no longer feels able to work for the banker.
- Bulstrode offers to settle the doctor's debts.

> **CONTEXT**
>
> The **epigraph** is from *Musophilus* (1599), a poetic dialogue by Samuel Daniel (1562–1619) written to assert the importance of education and of poetry in cultivating the values of a gentleman.

> **CONTEXT**
>
> The epigraph is from 'The Book of Sirach', also known as 'Ecclesiasticus', one of the apocryphal books of the Bible.

On the day Bulstrode refuses assistance to Lydgate, Garth visits the banker's office. He has encountered Raffles on the road, clearly very ill, and has taken him to Stone Court. Bulstrode sends for Lydgate. Garth declares himself unable to work for Bulstrode any more as Raffles has told him of the banker's past. Garth later informs his wife that he has detached himself from the taint of association with Bulstrode.

Bulstrode rides to Stone Court, anxious to arrive before Lydgate. Despite the disagreeable nature of their earlier conversation, the doctor complies with Bulstrode's request to attend the sick man. He diagnoses a serious but not fatal condition, and advocates constant monitoring and total abstinence from alcohol. Bulstrode decides he should look after the patient personally.

While returning to his home, Lydgate considers with dread the prospect before him. Arriving, he finds an inventory of his possessions is being taken. Rosamond has taken to her bed. She is persuaded not to return to her parents, but the marriage is immensely strained.

COMMENTARY

Bulstrode takes comfort from the fact that his secret has been exposed to Garth and not some less discreet person. Earlier, he felt justifiably confident that Ladislaw would not disclose any details of his past. But he recognises the need to limit the damage Raffles may cause, and under the guise of offering altruistic assistance towards a sick man, and to the financially troubled doctor, he endeavours to protect his self-interest (see **Themes: Altruism and egotism**).

CHAPTER 70

- Raffles dies.
- Lydgate is uneasy at the circumstances surrounding the death, but Bulstrode agrees to lend him money to pay his his bills.
- Lydgate is relieved that his immediate financial difficulties have been resolved.

Bulstrode examines the contents of Raffles's pockets to trace his previous whereabouts. Then he sits with the sleeping man. Next morning, Lydgate leaves opium to be administered in small doses if Raffles becomes sleepless. Bulstrode writes a cheque to cover the doctor's debts. That evening he entrusts Raffles to the care of Mrs Abel, his housekeeper, but deliberately neglects to specify the limit of the dosage. He also gives her the key to his wine-cooler where brandy is kept. Next morning, Lydgate arrives in time to witness the death of Raffles. He feels uneasy about the circumstances, but says nothing.

At home, Lydgate is visited by Farebrother, who has grown concerned about the doctor's uncharacteristic behaviour. He is astonished to find Lydgate cheerful. The doctor tells the rector that Bulstrode has advanced him money to pay his bills. Privately, he is unsettled by his awareness that Bulstrode's change of heart was followed so swiftly by the death in his house, but he talks of his plans to economise and ensure a brighter future.

COMMENTARY

It is again apparent that character is not simply a fixed entity, but is shaped by circumstances, and is inaccurately assessed if considered in isolation from changing contexts. Farebrother takes the lesson on board; in Chapter 72 he observes that 'character is not cut in marble – it is not something solid and unalterable. It is something living and changing, and may become diseased as our bodies do' (pp. 734–5) (see **Characterisation**).

 QUESTION

Who do you think should be considered responsible for Raffles's death? Lydgate, who supplied the opium? Mrs Abel, who administered the fatal dose in combination with alcohol? Bulstrode, who withheld vital information? Or Raffles himself, who destroyed his own health through excessive drinking?

CHAPTER 71

- Bambridge, the horse-dealer, has heard from Raffles the story of Bulstrode's disreputable past. He spreads the news.
- Bulstrode is forced to resign from public positions.
- Dorothea determines to restore Lydgate's reputation, which has been tarnished by association.

Outside the Green Dragon, the horse-dealer Bambridge informs his friends that at Bilkley horse-fair he heard Raffles tell how Bulstrode had acquired his wealth. Hopkins, the draper, exclaims that he has recently furnished Raffles's funeral at Bulstrode's expense. Others gather round to hear the story elaborated.

Frank Hawley, a lawyer and town-clerk, speaks of the matter with Farebrother. Farebrother perceives an unwelcome association between Lydgate's relief from debt and his service to Bulstrode in attending Raffles. Connections are made less sympathetically by others, and gossip concerning the banker's alliance with the doctor spreads through Middlemarch.

A meeting is convened to discuss the town's response to a case of cholera. Bulstrode and Lydgate happen to arrive together. There is a call for Bulstrode's resignation from public positions, on account of the allegations levelled by Raffles. Lydgate helps the suddenly frail banker leave the room, while feeling bitterness at his own perceived guilt by association. After the meeting, Brooke, accompanied by Farebrother, drives to see Dorothea. Both are concerned about the position in which Lydgate has been placed. Dorothea insists that they should actively seek to clear Lydgate's name.

COMMENTARY

Despite Bulstrode's precautions, gossip spreads, forming a web which traps him, and also ensnares Lydgate. Speculation is woven around the basic facts and produces various interpretations, but predominantly these denigrate the reputations of both men.

At the start of Chapter 41 the **narrator** remarks that this world is 'apparently a huge whispering-gallery' (p. 412). The image **alludes** to galleries built, generally under domes, in a way that allows whispers to be heard clearly in other parts of the building; for example, in St Paul's Cathedral, London. Figuratively, it alludes to the spreading of scandal. Here, in Chapter 71, we see vividly how gossip is generated, elaborated, and spread – the whispering-gallery at work.

GLOSSARY

716 **Botany Bay** penal colony in Australia

725 **Act of Parliament** passed in July 1828, making provision for improved sanitation as a public health measure

CHAPTER 72

- Dorothea urges action on behalf of Lydgate.

Dorothea is dissatisfied with Farebrother's 'cautious weighing of consequences' in relation to Lydgate. She would prefer 'ardent faith in efforts of justice and mercy' (p. 733). Over dinner with the rector and the Chettams, she asks 'What do we live for, if it is not to make life less difficult to each other?' (pp. 733–4). Chettam insists that Lydgate must act for himself. Dorothea, discouraged by the company, bursts into tears.

COMMENTARY

Dorothea's **rhetorical question**, 'What do we live for, if it is not to make life less difficult to each other?', shows that her idealism has survived her unfortunate marriage. It has always been combined with practical altruism, in her plans to build cottages, and now, on a more personal basis, in her determination to restore Lydgate's reputation as an honourable man.

CHAPTER 73

- Lydgate considers likely consequences of the loss of Bulstrode's reputation.

After taking Bulstrode home, Lydgate rides several miles out of Middlemarch to think matters over. He deduces the truth of Bulstrode's situation. He also comprehends how he is now viewed by the people of Middlemarch. He resolves to defend his honour and to stand by Bulstrode, but he feels weighed down with anticipation of Rosamond's reaction.

COMMENTARY

The **narrator** offers a sympathetic view of Lydgate's plight:

> Only those who know the supremacy of the intellectual life – the life which has a seed of ennobling thought and purpose within it – can understand the grief of one who falls from that serene activity into the absorbing soul-wasting struggle with worldly annoyances. (p. 737)

Practical characters, such as Caleb Garth and his daughter, appear in a positive light in *Middlemarch*. They are well equipped to deal resourcefully with life's daily challenges. Those who aspire to loftier achievements are frustrated and damaged by such 'annoyances'.

The Garths keep the world on an even keel, but the idealists aspire to improve it. Invariably, such idealism is eventually compromised. Dorothea will become a wife and mother. Lydgate will give up research and become a successful practitioner. Still, in George Eliot's view, each spark of idealism moves the world forward a little.

CHAPTER 74

CONTEXT

The **epigraph** is from the 'Book of Tobit', an apocryphal book of the Bible.

- Mrs Bulstrode learns of her husband's disgrace.
- She adopts simple dress, and pledges her loyalty to him.

Rosamond and her aunt, Mrs Bulstrode, are implicated in local gossip. Mrs Bulstrode has felt unsettled about her husband since he brought Raffles home, and she asks Lydgate whether anything untoward has happened. He gives nothing away, so she goes to town in search of news. Eventually, Vincy, her brother spells out her misfortune. People will talk, whatever the truth may be. He wishes they had never heard of Bulstrode or Lydgate.

Back home, Mrs Bulstrode retires to her room, entrusting care of her husband to her daughters. She changes her clothes, dressing now with plain simplicity. When she rejoins her husband, his anguish is palpable, and she feels compassionate and tender towards him. They shed tears together: 'His confession was silent, and her promise of faithfulness was silent' (p. 750).

COMMENTARY

Mrs Bulstrode's loyalty to her husband appears admirable, especially when compared with the way her niece has responded to problems in her marriage with Lydgate. But when she adopts simple dress as an act of humility, we may recall the demands of loyalty made upon Dorothea by Casaubon. In that light, the supporting role allocated to wives may appear repressive, and Mrs Bulstrode's self-sacrificing compliance may appear less worthy of unquestioning respect.

CHAPTER 75

- Rosamond's spirits are lifted by clearance of Lydgate's debts and news of Ladislaw's imminent arrival.
- Then, she hears of the scandal surrounding Bulstrode and her husband. She is devastated.

Once the immediate financial threat has been lifted, Lydgate seeks to mend his marriage. Rosamond feels unfulfilled, and is keen to move to London. Dissatisfied at home, her thoughts turn to the alluringly romantic figure of Will Ladislaw. When a letter arrives from Ladislaw, indicating that he will soon visit Middlemarch, Rosamond's spirits are lifted. She arranges a dinner party for friends, without telling Lydgate. The invitations are declined. Lydgate is furious when he finds out what has happened.

> **CONTEXT**
>
> Newgate (p. 743) was a bleak old London prison. The social reformer Elizabeth Fry (1780–1845) was so appalled at conditions within the building that in 1817 she helped found an Association for the Reformation of the Female Prisoners in Newgate and agitated tirelessly for more wide-ranging prison reforms. Newgate was eventually closed in 1902 and demolished two years later.

> **CONTEXT**
>
> The epigraph translates as 'Inconstancy arises from the feeling that present pleasures are false and from lack of awareness of the vanity of absent pleasures.' As with the epigraph for Chapter 30, it is from Pascal's *Pensées* (Thoughts).

Feeling hurt, Rosamond visits her parents, who disclose the scandal of Bulstrode and its implications for Lydgate. Rosamond is now adamant that she and her husband must move to London.

COMMENTARY

Rosamond's response to her husband's troubles contrasts dramatically with that of her aunt in the previous chapter. It is tempting to see Mrs Bulstrode in a positive light, and to cast Rosamond in negative terms. But Mrs Bulstrode's upbringing results in obedient compliance, while Rosamond's education has led her to expect social advancement as a reward for her feminine charm. Her disobedience, like her aunt's loyalty, results from a well defined view of the social role of women. The extremes they seem to represent may be closer together than is immediately apparent.

CHAPTER 76

- Dorothea offers support to Lydgate.

A few days later, Lydgate is summoned to Lowick Manor. Dorothea wishes to support the hospital. She is struck by the change in his looks. Lydgate reveals he may be leaving Middlemarch. She praises his integrity, and asks him to explain the circumstances which led to harmful gossip. He welcomes an opportunity to speak with a benevolent friend, and tells his side of the story.

Dorothea offers to support his work, in the hope that one day his reputation will transcend the damage done by scandal. He speaks of his obligations to his wife, who now fervently wishes to leave the area. Dorothea volunteers to speak with her, affirming her own desire to assist his 'power to do great things' (p. 767). She writes a cheque for one thousand pounds, enabling Lydgate to clear his debt to Bulstrode.

COMMENTARY

The narrative has affirmed an underlying affinity between Dorothea and Lydgate: both are idealists who wish to help others, especially the less fortunate, and both become trapped in unfortunate marriages. As a woman, Dorothea does not feel able to aspire to greatness through her own actions but she continues to hope that she can help a man 'do great things' (p. 767). She speaks with a 'child-like grave-eyed earnestness' (p. 765), indicative of her acceptance of the superior capabilities of men. Lydgate will not achieve greatness, but George Eliot believed that even unsuccessful striving produces small changes towards gradual social improvement.

CHAPTER 77

- Dorothea finds Ladislaw alone with Rosamond.

> **CONTEXT**
>
> The epigraph is from Shakespeare's *Henry V*, Act II, Scene 2. The King is the speaker.

Next day, Lydgate goes to a nearby town called Brassing. Rosamond remains at home, melancholy, yet eagerly awaiting the arrival of Ladislaw.

Dorothea also has Ladislaw on her mind. His reputation locally has suffered from the disclosures concerning Bulstrode. Arriving at Lydgate's house, hoping to speak with Rosamond, she finds Ladislaw clasping the hands of the doctor's tearful wife. He is evidently moved at the sight of Dorothea, but she hurriedly explains she is delivering a letter for Lydgate, and retreats from the room. Overcoming her emotional turmoil, she visits Chettam and her uncle, intent upon clearing Lydgate's name.

COMMENTARY

In the preceding chapter, Dorothea pledged ardent support for Lydgate's work. Here, she is thrown into turmoil when she finds Ladislaw with the doctor's wife. The strength of her jealousy is a measure of the love she feels for Ladislaw, an emotional attachment of a different order to her respectful feelings for Lydgate.

CHAPTER 78

- Rosamond, feeling rejected by Ladislaw, displays greater warmth towards her husband.

QUESTION

The American novelist Henry James (1843–1916) declared George Eliot's depiction of Will Ladislaw to be, on the whole, a failure, lacking sharpness of definition and depth of colour. At this point do you find Will Ladislaw a sufficiently three dimensional character to support the role he has been assigned in such a large and ambitious novel?

After Dorothea's hasty departure, the atmosphere between Ladislaw and Rosamond is tense. He responds furiously to her sarcastic suggestion that he should pursue Dorothea and make plain his preference for her. Ladislaw has lost the consoling certainty that Dorothea believes in him, but his devotion to her is total: 'No other woman exists by the side of her' (p. 778). Rosamond is devastated to discover that far from being held high in his esteem, she is excluded from Ladislaw's deeper feelings. Suddenly, 'her little world was in ruins' (p. 780).

Lydgate returns home to find his wife lying on her bed in a state of distress. He comforts her, and senses an unaccustomed warmth in her response. He erroneously assumes this is the beneficial effect of Dorothea speaking on his behalf.

COMMENTARY

Ladislaw speaks to Rosamond with brutal frankness. This is a measure of his frustrated passion for Dorothea. It also has a salutary effect, as it breaks down the barrier of her egotism: 'What another nature felt in opposition to her own was being burnt and bitten into her consciousness' (p. 779). A degree of sympathy with others has been admitted, and this is manifested in her increased warmth towards Lydgate (see **Themes: Altruism and egotism**).

CHAPTER 79

- Lydgate talks with Ladislaw about the damage caused by their connections with Bulstrode.

Lydgate finds the letter left by Dorothea. Then Ladislaw arrives, and the doctor tells him that Rosamond is unwell. Lydgate speaks of the scandal which has degraded his own and Ladislaw's reputation within Middlemarch. He notes a change in Ladislaw's demeanour when Dorothea is mentioned, and suspects that she is the real reason for his presence in the locality. He projects a future in which their friendship will be renewed in London.

COMMENTARY

Ladislaw has rejected Bulstrode's offer of financial assistance and believes he has cut himself free. Lydgate, on the other hand, has accepted the banker's money. The crucial difference lies in their circumstances, rather than in strength of character. Both men aspire to improve the world around them, both are intolerant of pettiness and ignorance, and both are anxious about the prospects for their high aspirations:

> We are on a perilous margin when we begin to look passively at our future selves, and see our own figures led with dull consent into insipid misdoing and shabby achievement. Poor Lydgate was inwardly groaning on that margin, and Will was arriving at it. (p. 783)

CHAPTER 80

- Dorothea continues to defend Lydgate, and grows increasingly aware of her love for Ladislaw.

Dorothea dines with Farebrother and his family, and takes the opportunity to explain that Lydgate has been a victim of circumstance. Mention of Ladislaw flusters her, and she leaves hastily. At home, alone, she is overcome with grief and tearfully she moans, 'Oh, I did love him!' (p. 786).

Next day she forces herself to relive the previous day's experiences. She feels that she has been unjust to Rosamond, whom she was

---

CONTEXT

The **epigraph** is from *The Pilgrim's Progress* (1678) by John Bunyan (1628–88). This **allegorical** work tells of the journey of an ordinary man named Christian from his home to the heavenly Celestial City. At this point, he falls into the Slough of Despond – a physical swamp in Bunyan's allegory; a state of despair, in psychological terms.

CONTEXT

The epigraph is from 'Ode to Duty' (1805) by William Wordsworth (1770–1850).

intending to enlighten and support. Looking from her window, she sees the early morning stirrings of working people, and ponders 'the largeness of the world and the manifold wakings of men to labour and endurance' (p. 788).

She instructs Tantripp to bring her new dress, and lays aside her more sombre mourning garments. She then walks towards Middlemarch, intent on helping Rosamond Lydgate.

COMMENTARY

Dorothea feels helpless in her love for Ladislaw, and cries like a child. But that suggestion of immature dependency contrasts with the mature capacity for sympathy she then demonstrates. 'Was she alone in the scene? Was it her event only?' (p. 787) she asks, forcing herself to pass beyond her own subjectivity and see matters from the points of view of the other participants.

Looking from her window she sees people starting work, and the range of her sympathies is extended still further: 'She was a part of that involuntary, palpitating life, and could neither look out on it from her luxurious shelter as a mere spectator, nor hide her eyes in selfish complaining' (p. 788). Recent chapters have focused closely upon the entangled lives of Dorothea and Ladislaw, Lydgate and Rosamond. Here Dorothea looks out into the world again and resolves to live actively. Fresh clothes are an outward indication of that resolve.

CHAPTER 81

- Dorothea speaks with Rosamond of Lydgate's integrity, and is told of Ladislaw's love for her.

Lydgate is preparing to leave when Dorothea arrives at his house. He gives her a letter, offering thanks for her generous assistance, and leaves her to talk with his wife.

Rosamond is anxious, but Dorothea clasps her hand with 'gentle motherliness' (p. 793), and speaks with 'self-forgetful ardour' (p. 795) in defence of Lydgate's character and behaviour. Rosamond sobs. Dorothea speaks of the peculiar obligations which marriage brings. They embrace, then Rosamond declares that Dorothea is mistaken in her interpretation of the previous day's events. She reveals that Ladislaw declared his total commitment to love for Dorothea.

Lydgate returns, and Dorothea leaves the couple to rebuild their relationship.

COMMENTARY

Speaking with Lydgate, Dorothea appeared 'child-like'. When counselling Rosamond her 'motherliness' surfaces. Her decision to act, rather than remain passive, has brought her maturity. She is 'self-forgetful' when she defends Lydgate. That capacity to transcend egotism is a lesson which Rosamond needs to learn, and the embrace between the women suggests that learning process has begun (see **Themes: Altruism and egotism**).

CHAPTER 82

- Ladislaw learns that his love for Dorothea is reciprocated.

After a day away from Middlemarch, Ladislaw returns to spend a discomforting evening with the Lydgates. He returns to his hotel room and reluctantly reads a note passed to him by Rosamond. It indicates that all has been explained to Dorothea, who consequently holds him once again in high esteem.

COMMENTARY

Rosamond's note is a 'self-forgetful' gesture, showing that she has learnt sympathy from Dorothea. Her discretion, in committing the message to paper rather than blurting it out, shows a mature understanding lacking from her earlier actions.

CONTEXT

The **epigraph** translates as 'You too, Earth, have remained unshaken this night, / And now you breathe refreshed at my feet, / Stirring new joys around me, / Stirring a strong new resolution within me: /constantly to strive for life's highest goals.' It is from the tragic drama *Faust, Part Two* (1832) by Johann Wolfgang von Goethe (1749–1832).

CONTEXT

The epigraph is from Shakespeare's 'Sonnet 50'.

GLOSSARY

803 **the Rubicon** stream in Italy. In 48BC, Julius Caesar crossed it with his army. This was taken as a declaration of war. 'To cross the Rubicon' consequently means to take an irrevocable step

CHAPTER 83

• Ladislaw visits Dorothea at Lowick Manor. They declare their love for one another.

Miss Noble – Farebrother's aunt – arrives at Lowick Manor, a go-between from Ladislaw, who wishes to see Dorothea. Soon, Ladislaw appears in the library. He proclaims his devotion to Dorothea and kisses her hand. She is visibly moved.

Outside there is a storm. The couple smile at one another, and talk with an underlying sense that their love is hopeless. They hold hands 'like two children' (p. 810). They kiss, then move apart. Ladislaw is furious with frustration that they can never be married. When he says goodbye, Dorothea cries out that she hates her wealth, and says that if he leaves her heart will break. He holds her in his arms, and she affirms that they can live well on her own inheritance.

COMMENTARY

The breaking of the storm can be seen as **symbolic** of the lovers' suppressed passion rising to the surface. The couple are compared to children, suggesting their feeling of helplessness. This is overcome because Dorothea is decisive. She insists that her future will be with Ladislaw, and that she will surrender Lowick Manor. The adjective 'queenly' is applied to her in these concluding chapters, indicating that she has taken control of events, for the moment at least.

CHAPTER 84

• Dorothea's family and friends are distressed at her engagement to Ladislaw, but she refuses to change her mind.

Mr Cadwallader walks with Chettam on the lawn at Freshitt Hall. Mrs Cadwallader talks with Celia and Chettam's mother. Brooke arrives. It is assumed that his evident dejection has been caused by the failure of the Reform Bill, but he reveals that its source is actually Dorothea's decision to marry Ladislaw in three weeks time. The news is received with disbelief.

Celia goes to Lowick to try to exert sisterly influence. Dorothea is delighted to see her, but rejects her advice. Celia points out that they will not be able to meet after the marriage, on account of Chettam's disapproval. Dorothea plans to move to London with Ladislaw.

COMMENTARY

Middlemarch conveys a sense of historical process at work, in which local communities are increasingly drawn under the influence of centralised power. There are many references to Acts of Parliament, passed in London but extending their influence out into the provinces. Meanwhile, the emergent growth of the railway network establishes new social relationships between previously unconnected communities.

Still, individuals are faced with their own choices, judgements, and dilemmas. Brooke has Reform on his mind, but he also feels highly personal concern about Dorothea's decision to marry Ladislaw. It is a major part of George Eliot's achievement in this novel to hold together the personal and the historical within the same **narrative** frame.

CHAPTER 85

- Bulstrode prepares to leave Middlemarch.
- His wife asks him to help Vincy's family.
- He asks her to persuade Garth to resume supervision of Stone Court.

CONTEXT

After the defeat of the initial Reform Bill in March 1831 two further Reform Bills were presented to Parliament before the Reform Act, introducing wide-ranging changes to the electoral system, was eventually passed in June 1832.

GLOSSARY

814 **Draco … Jeffreys** Draco, who lived in the seventh century BC, and Judge Jeffreys (1648–89) were notorious for their judicial severity

CONTEXT

The **epigraph** is from *The Pilgrim's Progress* (1678) by John Bunyan (1628–88). Note how the **narrator** makes direct reference to the quotation in order to focus our awareness of Bulstrode's situation.

Bulstrode prepares to leave Middlemarch, haunted by the sense that he is not the man he has pretended to be. He dreads that his wife might come to perceive him as a murderer. Their daughters have been sent away to boarding school to shield them from the crisis. Mrs Bulstrode asks her husband to assist her brother's family. He points out that Lydgate, Vincy's son-in-law, is unlikely to accept help, as he returned the previous loan. Mrs Bulstrode recognises the moral rejection implied by that settled debt, and weeps.

Bulstrode suggests that Fred might be helped if Garth could be persuaded to assume management of Stone Court. He indicates that persuasion must come from his wife.

COMMENTARY

Bulstrode's habitual selfishness has been broken down. At last, he manifests concern for the well-being of others (see **Themes: Altruism and egotism**).

CHAPTER 86

- Caleb Garth tells Mary that Fred Vincy can become manager of Stone Court.
- Mary breaks the news to Fred.

Mary is in the garden when Caleb Garth arrives home. They discuss her love for Fred Vincy. He then announces that Fred may live at Stone Court, overseeing it for his aunt Bulstrode. This would enable the young couple to marry. Fred arrives, and Garth leaves Mary to convey the news to him.

COMMENTARY

It is appropriate that the honest and practical Garth family occupies the concluding chapter. They are a touchstone for decency and integrity, even though lofty thoughts are alien to them.

CONTEXT

The **epigraph** translates as 'The heart is saturated with love as with a divine salt which preserves it; from this springs the unswerving devotion of those who have loved one another since the dawning of life, and the freshness of old, enduring loves. There is an embalming of love. [The young lovers] Daphnis and Chlöe become [the elderly couple] Philemon and Baucis. Such an old age is like an evening that resembles daybreak.' It is from the novel *L'homme qui rit* (The man who laughs) (1869), by the French writer Victor Hugo (1802–85).

FINALE

- Fred Vincy and Mary Garth are happily and successfully married.
- Lydgate achieves a degree of professional success and has a family with Rosamond, but he dies relatively young.
- Ladislaw becomes a Member of Parliament; Dorothea immerses herself in philanthropy and in the role of mother.
- Dorothea and Celia's children grow up as good friends, healing family divisions brought about by Dorothea's choice of husbands.

> **CONTEXT**
>
> The Municipal Corporations Act (see p. 836), passed in 1835, was a further step in progressive electoral Reform. It required that members of town councils should be elected by local taxpayers and that those councils should make public their financial records.

Fred and Mary's marriage results in 'a solid mutual happiness' (p. 832). Fred achieves distinction as a farmer. Mary publishes a book of stories, written initially for her three sons.

Lydgate dies at fifty, after establishing an excellent practice and writing a treatise on gout. He provides handsomely for his wife and four children. Rosamond subsequently marries a wealthy, elderly physician.

Dorothea never regrets giving up her fortune to marry Will Ladislaw. She remains actively philanthropic, while being both wife and mother. Ladislaw becomes a reforming Member of Parliament. Brooke keeps in correspondence with the rebellious couple, and an invitation to visit Tipton Grange, coinciding with news that Dorothea has given birth to a son, helps heal the family rift. Brooke lives into old age, then leaves his estate to Dorothea's son.

 QUESTION

Middlemarch has drawn us into the lives of this cast of characters through a prolonged and detailed **narrative**. Do you find that this summary overview works effectively as a concluding chapter?

Chettam always deplores the marriage to Ladislaw, a view shared by Middlemarch public opinion which disparages both of Dorothea's marriages. But the children of Dorothea Ladislaw and Celia Chettam grow up to be good friends.

COMMENTARY

The **narrator** surveys the subsequent course of lives delineated in the novel. Literary **realism** aims to satisfy readers' desire for knowledge. The concluding overview fortifies the illusion that these characters exist beyond the pages of a book.

George Eliot affirms through her narrator that gradual social improvement is not brought about solely by the great. Unacknowledged contributions are made by those who act with genuine sympathy and compassion for others. Dorothea's influence is difficult to calculate, 'for the growing good of the world is partly dependent on unhistoric acts; and that things are not so ill with you and me as they might have been, is half owing to the number who lived faithfully to a hidden life, and rest in unvisited tombs' (p. 838).

EXTENDED COMMENTARIES

TEXT 1 – CHAPTER 27, PAGES 264–5

From 'Let the high Muse ...' to '... his interest in the case'

This passage is from the start of Chapter 27. Lydgate is attending the sick Fred Vincy, an event that allows Rosamond to see more of the doctor.

**CHECK
THE POEM**
Compare the
distinction made in
George Eliot's
epigraph with the
meditation on Art
and Life in the
famous 'Ode on a
Grecian Urn' (1819)
by John Keats
(1795–1821).

The passage begins with an **epigraph** of the kind which heads every chapter. Each epigraph focuses our attention upon a particular issue which will feature in the following pages. Unlike the majority, this is not an attributed quotation, but was invented by George Eliot. It affirms that her concerns are with human events in history, rather than with the Olympian gods of Greek **myth**.

It is a point to which she returns on the novel's last page, where she refers to the Christian saint Theresa, and the classical heroine Antigone. They were models of noble self-sacrifice, and Dorothea is regularly compared to both throughout *Middlemarch*. But at the end of the story the **narrator** laments that 'the medium in which their ardent deeds took shape is for ever gone' (p. 838). Eliot is committed to a **realist** mode of writing about the lives of ordinary human beings, rather than the exceptional creatures of myth and **legend**.

After the epigraph, the narrator **alludes** to a personal friend, an 'eminent philosopher'. The **narrative voice** assumes a human form at such points; it announces that it has a life beyond the telling of this story. It is tempting to identify the narrator with George Eliot, who knew prominent thinkers of the day, such as John Tyndall and Herbert Spencer. But it would be naive to overlook the artifice involved in composing the narrative voice, and it is difficult to identify it consistently with the author.

George Eliot's contemporaries would have assumed that the 'eminent philosopher' was a man. Philosophy, the domain of abstract thought, was conventionally masculine. Mention of the housemaid (on p. 264) indicates that within a patriarchal society less elevated tasks, such as housework, are allocated to lower class women.

George Eliot, going against the patriarchal grain, was fascinated by contemporary science and that interest furnished the striking image which follows. We are told that a lighted candle, placed against the surface of a mirror, will arrange haphazard scratches on that surface into a regular concentric pattern. Order emerges from chaos. But the effect is an illusion, created by 'exclusive optical selection' (p. 264). The basic scientific experiment is then translated into terms of human understanding, and applied to the story being told. The scratches represent random events in the world; the candle represents a sentient being discerning pattern in the randomness. The self (in this case Rosamond Vincy's self) perceives order, and acts in accordance with that perception. The truth is, however, that the order is illusory.

The word 'Providence' is introduced, as it frequently is in *Middlemarch*, to invoke the orthodox Christian view that God has an all-encompassing plan which grants meaning to the world. George Eliot, along with a significant number of other Victorian intellectuals, had lost faith in that divine provision. The word is used **ironically**, reducing it to the trivial status of a purely personal perception of order in the world: 'Rosamond had a Providence of her own who had kindly made her more charming than other girls' (p. 264).

> **CONTEXT**
>
> John Tyndall (1820–93) was an Irish scientist with wide ranging interests. He investigated the impact of glaciers, and did important work in the disparate fields of thermodynamics and microbiology. Herbert Spencer (1820–1903) was an influential English philosopher and political theorist who, under the influence of Charles Darwin's writings, championed the cause of evolutionary theory and coined the phrase 'survival of the fittest'.

Casaubon's search for the key to all mythologies, and Lydgate's quest for the primitive tissue from which all others derive, may be seen as lighted candles placed against the scratched pier-glass of human existence. Both men wish to discover the sun around which the concentric circles have formed in their respective fields of study, to uncover the order which underpins their understanding. The **parable** offered here suggests that the sun is simply their own perception of pattern, not something detectable outside of themselves. They both labour under an illusion concerning the nature of human knowledge, and their failure is inevitable.

On a more mundane level, we can see that Rosamond's self-centredness limits sympathy for others. Her brother's illness does not cause her great anxiety, but is a welcome occasion for her to exert influence over Lydgate. Her concern for her mother's well-being is, at least in part, motivated by her desire to make a favourable impression upon the doctor. It is not until her discussion with Dorothea in Chapter 81 that Rosamond learns to consider events from the point of view of another person. Only then does it become possible for her to extend sympathy.

Mrs Vincy's response to Fred's illness is dramatically different. Her son, in his early twenties, has caused disappointment and anxiety on account of his idleness and lack of direction. But now he 'was one with the babe whom she had loved, with a love new to her, before he was born' (p. 265). Circumstances have transformed the mother's perception; tolerant affection has given way to an idealised vision. Evaluation of other people is always modified by changes in the emotional state of the perceiver. This is nowhere more evident than in the shift from Ladislaw's detached amusement at the prospect of Dorothea's marriage, in Chapter 9, to his later impassioned assessment of her as a perfect woman and a goddess descended to earth.

Middlemarch shows that the course of an individual life is unpredictable. It can be affected in a major way by events that might appear incidental to it. So, Fred Vincy's debts led him to travel to the horse-fair where he contracted fever. The Vincys were dissatisfied with Mr Wrench's treatment of their son, so Lydgate,

CONTEXT

The consolidation of democracy and advancement of the middle classes in nineteenth-century England prompted serious thought about the nature of individual greatness and the qualities required for leadership. It became a central concern for essayist and historian Thomas Carlyle (1795–1881), especially in his book *On Heroes and Hero Worship and the Heroic in History* (1841).

who happened to be nearby, was summoned to attend him. Lydgate is attracted to Rosamond physically, and is impressed by her show of considerateness. They subsequently marry and his aspiration to accomplish important research is constrained by the material demands of domestic life.

TEXT 2 – CHAPTER 39, PAGES 389–90

From 'And you are going to engage Mr Garth ...' to '... away very cheerfully.'

In this passage, which takes place mid way through the novel, Dorothea is talking with her uncle, attempting to persuade him to make improvements in the living conditions of his tenants. Will Ladislaw is also present. Dorothea is aware that Brooke has been justly criticised for allowing his estate to deteriorate, while presenting himself as a reforming politician. She also sees an opportunity to realise at Tipton a plan for building cottages like those now built at Freshitt. Her altruism contrasts with his own limited vision, which is blinkered by self-interest.

Dorothea speaks with directness and fluency, which reflect her commitment. Indeed, she is compared to a choirboy singing a 'credo' (p. 389), a declaration of faith. The **simile** suggests her childlike innocence, and the religious passion which animates her very practical suggestions. Brooke, contrastingly, speaks with equivocation, unsure of his own position. His utterances are always far from fluent, displaying muddled thinking. He habitually includes the phrase 'you know', a verbal tic which soon becomes meaningless, while ostensibly referring to shared knowledge. It serves to emphasise Brooke's own debilitating lack of insight. His consciousness is reduced to 'a stammering condition under the eloquence of his niece' (p. 390). George Eliot regularly uses contrast of this kind, developing characterisation by emphasising difference.

Dorothea is not only aware of the conditions endured by her uncle's tenants, she actually refers to those tenants by name. One of the themes of *Middlemarch* is the relationship between the general and the particular. Dorothea is devoted to ideas, and abides by general principles, but she also pays attention to specific details, showing

CHECK THE BOOK

The protagonist of George Eliot's novel *Silas Marner* (1861) is a weaver living in a village. That novel also addresses the impact of industrialisation upon more traditional methods of working.

CONTEXT

Cottage building schemes were a notable aspect of philanthropy in nineteenth century England. Upper class landowners would provide cottages to house workers on their estates. This may have been to some extent an altruistic act but it also served to improve the appearance of their property and helped to defuse potential discontent and unrest amongst their workforce.

CHECK THE BOOK

An interesting account can be found in 'The Cottage Homes of England', the second chapter in John Burnett's *A Social History of Housing, 1815–1985* (Routledge, 1986). Burnett notes that 'cottage improvement remained exceptional, if not eccentric, and its products stood out as isolated oases in the general desert of neglect' (p. 53).

CHECK THE BOOK

An informative account of the status of classical education during this period, and of subsequent changes to that status, can be found in Christopher Stray's *Classics Transformed: Schools, Universities, and Society in England 1830–1960* (Clarendon Press, 1998).

sympathetic interest in particular cases. This grants her a moral astuteness which is not allowed by either principles or details alone. Later, Lydgate uses scientific terms to convey the need for such flexible vision: 'a man's mind must be continually expanding and shrinking between the whole human horizon and the horizon of an object-glass' (p. 640).

Dorothea is critical of the 'simpering pictures' her uncle favours. She criticises the 'wicked attempt to find delight in what is false' (p. 389) which they represent, in her view. George Eliot took pains to write responsible realist fiction, avoiding 'that softening influence of the fine arts which make other people's hardships picturesque' (p. 393). She was wary of dealing with issues that readers might find offensive – her handling of Rigg's illegitimacy is notably cautious – but she is careful in *Middlemarch* to steer clear of sentimentality. She exposes hardships endured by the labouring class, but she does not idealise the farm workers.

Dorothea's marriage to Casaubon is described as 'a perpetual struggle of energy with fear' (p. 389). This is an abstract way to describe a woman's battle to overcome her sense of intimidation within a marriage, but it is a highly effective means of disclosing **epic** conflicts occurring beneath the surface of provincial life. Dorothea's frustration is in this way projected as a struggle conceived in terms that have universal significance. All human beings know fear, while energy is a basic requirement of existence.

Listening to Dorothea speak, Ladislaw recognises 'a certain greatness' in her, which leaves him with 'a chilling sense of remoteness' (p. 389). The **narrator** suggests that nature has 'intended greatness for men', adding with telling **irony** that in the case of Mr Brooke nature had failed in that intention. The irony undermines that sense of a natural order in which men are necessarily superior. The electoral speech Brooke later delivers is a disaster. That is not surprising given his lack of oratorical prowess. But Dorothea's persuasiveness and articulateness seem contrary to what was required of women in Victorian England, and Ladislaw is struck by the way she transcends the limits imposed by her gender.

His high estimation of her is fuelled by admiration of that capacity to rise above her condition.

Brooke's bumbling manner is endearing at the start of the novel, but it appears increasingly irresponsible and the product of selfishness. He patronises Dorothea, saying 'you understand a little Latin now' (p. 390). She has conscientiously sought to compensate for her lack of classical education in order to do serious work with Casaubon. Brooke throws in a familiar Latin phrase which can scarcely be taken as proof of his own erudition. He suggests that young ladies are 'a little one-sided', but Dorothea's capacity to see things from more than one point of view contrasts starkly with his own incapacity to do so.

A footman arrives to announce that the gamekeeper has caught a poacher. The culprit is a member of the Dagley family to which Dorothea has just referred, and the crime is a clear indication of the hard times the family is experiencing. Brooke is a magistrate, accustomed to dealing with such transgressors. In Chapter 4 there is reference to 'poor Bunch', a sheep-stealer condemned to be hanged for his offence, despite Brooke's efforts to secure a pardon. He declares he will be lenient with young Dagley. Brooke is essentially well-meaning, but tends to be insensitive and morally short-sighted.

> **CONTEXT**
>
> One of the functions of gamekeepers, employed by landowners to manage the wildlife on their estates, is to prevent poaching of game. Punishment was severe during the early years of the nineteenth century; some poachers were hanged. Under the Night Poaching Act, passed by Parliament in 1828, offenders might be imprisoned or transported to Australia as convicts.

TEXT 3 – CHAPTER 56, PAGES 554–5

From 'In the absence of any precise idea …' to '… a centre of hostility to the country'.

This passage is from Chapter 56, where the widowed Dorothea has been showing her talent for business and enterprise by advising Caleb Garth on improving the land. The forthcoming railway is a subject of concern to the local people, especially those in the small hamlet of Frick, near to Middlemarch.

Setting *Middlemarch* forty years in the past, George Eliot was able to write with informed hindsight about the processes of social change that she had witnessed during her life. The advent of the railway network was a major technological development in

CHECK THE BOOK

An enjoyable and enlightening contemporary account of rural England is William Cobbett's *Rural Rides* (1830) (Penguin Books, 2005). Cobbett (1763–1835) was a farmer and journalist sympathetic to Reform. His book documents his travels on horseback in the south of England and the Midlands, during the 1820s, and includes observations on the plight of the agricultural poor and the impact of innovations such as the threshing machine.

Victorian England. During the 1840s it grew very rapidly. One of the first main lines connected London with Birmingham, the major city in the English Midlands. Steam locomotives developed rapidly too. The country was in effect reconfigured by the railway map; remote places were connected, and journeys could be made faster than on the old stagecoach routes. The railway changed relationships in time and space as its network extended across the country.

In this passage George Eliot creates a group of rural working men who voice opposition to this new and entirely unfamiliar technology: 'In the absence of any precise idea as to what railways were, public opinion in Frick was against them' (p. 554). *Middlemarch* registers middle class agitation for reform in numerous areas of social life; it also indicates resistance to change, especially amongst the working poor. While businessmen prospered workers had often found their labour devalued during the preceding decades by the arrival of new and efficient industrial machinery. Despite the narrator's allusion to a 'proverbial tendency to admire the unknown' (p. 554), George Eliot repeatedly shows conservative distrust of innovation and change to be widespread. Social change may bring long term benefits but it can cause great disruption and hardship in the process.

Frick is an isolated hamlet, where life runs slowly and horizons are extremely narrow. The focus of attention for these local men is on the cost of food to fatten a pig, the price of beer in the local pub, the wages they might be paid by local farmers during the hard winter months. These are immediate, practical concerns.

The **narrator** says that they have no 'millennial expectations' (p. 554); that is, they hold no expectation of sudden, radical, and positive transformation in the conditions of their lives, such as that foreseen by the German philosophers Karl Marx (1818–83) and Frederick Engels (1820–95) in their *Communist Manifesto* (1848). Remember that *Middlemarch* is set forty years after the French Revolution of 1789, a major social upheaval that precipitated much violence.

There is a contrast between the 'strong muscular suspicion' (p. 555), which is the habitual outlook of these down-to-earth men, accustomed to being exploited and disappointed, and the idealistic benevolence of Dorothea Brooke, whose own material circumstances are so much more comfortable.

Solomon Featherstone, as a landowner and as overseer of the roads, has a vested interest in raising opposition to the railways. He seeks to shape 'the mind of Frick' (p. 555). *Middlemarch* is crucially concerned with perception of events from multiple points of view, but it is also concerned with consensus – points of view coinciding in shared understanding or belief, as here in the collective mind of this tiny community.

Immediately before this passage, Frick is described as 'a little centre of slow, heavy-shouldered industry' (p. 554). Featherstone is here described as a man 'who had an agreeable sense that he could afford to be slow' (p. 555). Before long the railways, heralding modern life, will speed things up and alter an entire way of life.

This passage includes some use of **dialect**. Hiram Ford, the waggoner, says 'Lunnon' (p. 555), meaning London. By the time *Middlemarch* was written education across the country was becoming increasingly standardised; it became still more so after the passing of the Elementary Education Act in 1870, and local differences in ways of speaking were gradually superseded by a more uniform English. Regional differences remain today, but the idiosyncrasies of local speech patterns were incompatible with the demand for uniformity in basic educational standards.

CHECK THE BOOK

Forty years after George Eliot wrote *Middlemarch* the English novelist E. M. Forster, in *Howard's End* (1910) (Penguin Books, 2000) wrote of a 'sense of flux' created by the railways. People were being uprooted from their locality and its traditions. England was becoming increasingly fluent and mobile in its ways of life. Forster goes on to observe provocatively: 'London was but a foretaste of this nomadic civilisation which is altering human nature so profoundly, and throws upon personal relations a stress greater than they have ever borne before.'

PART THREE

CRITICAL APPROACHES

CHECK THE BOOK

George Eliot's contemporary Charles Dickens was a master of description. Sketching a character he would sometimes verge on caricature in order to convey a vivid sense of a distinctive individual. See, for example, the description of Uncle Pumblechook in *Great Expectations* (1860–1), Chapter 4: 'a large hard-breathing middle-aged slow man, with a mouth like a fish, dull staring eyes, and sandy hair standing upright on his head, so that he looked as if he had just been all but choked, and had that moment come to'.

CHARACTERISATION

One of the basic assumptions of literary **realism** is that readers should feel they know the characters in a novel. Description of physical appearance plays its part; for example, we are told that Farebrother is 'a handsome, broad-chested but otherwise small man, about forty, whose black was very threadbare: the brilliancy was all in his quick grey eyes' (pp. 161–2). But there must be psychological coherence as well: behaviour should be explicable, and motives should be credible. George Eliot assists our understanding by contrasting different temperaments, as in the dialogues between Dorothea and Celia. Parallels also assist characterisation; an underlying affinity sheds light on both Dorothea and Lydgate.

Characterisation of individual figures is sustained with remarkable consistency throughout this long novel. The author's achievement is all the more striking as *Middlemarch* repeatedly asserts that character is not merely a fixed entity; it develops in response to circumstances, and may change according to context. The **narrator** affirms that character 'is a process and an unfolding' (p. 149). Farebrother observes that 'character is not cut in marble – it is not something solid and unalterable. It is something living and changing, and may become diseased as our bodies do' (pp. 734–5).

Linked to this point is another that complicates the rendering of character. George Eliot insists that an individual character should not be viewed in isolation, but as part of a web of social relationships. The point is distilled in the assertion that 'there is no creature whose inward being is so strong that it is not greatly determined by what lies outside it' (p. 838).

In addition, characters are subject to speculation or gossip, which offers an alternative interpretation of character and behaviour. This interpretation may be mistaken, yet still have significant impact on events. Dorothea's initial view of Casaubon prompts the narrator to remark:

> Signs are small measurable things, but interpretations are illimitable, and in girls of sweet, ardent nature, every sign is apt to conjure up wonder, hope, belief, vast as a sky, and coloured by a diffused thimbleful of matter in the shape of knowledge. (p. 25)

Lydgate, on the other hand, experiences difficulties, as an outsider in Middlemarch, partly because he is 'known merely as a cluster of signs for his neighbours' false suppositions' (p. 142). In fact, this idea that character is not fixed, and is made up of a series of impressions is a very modern one (see **Contemporary approaches: Post-structuralist criticism**).

Despite these complications, individual characters are drawn with sufficient clarity to enable summary:

ARTHUR BROOKE

Brooke, a country squire and magistrate around sixty years old, has never married, but is guardian to his nieces, Dorothea and Celia. His kindliness is combined with a rambling mind, reflected in his speech. His benevolent intentions are increasingly seen to be outweighed by problems arising from his self-absorption. Cadwallader describes him as 'a very good fellow, but pulpy; he will run into any mould, but he won't keep shape' (p. 70). This weakness is evident in his failure to alert Dorothea adequately to potential problems in her marriage to Casaubon. It is also evident in his political campaigning, which entirely lacks substance. He talks vaguely of Reform, while the living conditions of his own tenants deteriorate as a result of his meanness with money.

CELIA BROOKE

Affectionately called Kitty by her elder sister Dorothea, Celia is amiable, sensible, and agreeably direct. Those qualities win approval generally withheld from Dorothea's lofty aspirations. Her frank and good-humoured outlook often implies an **ironic** commentary upon her sister's scruples and ambitions. Celia makes the marriage which Dorothea declines, and she lives happily with Sir James Chettam and their children. Her contentment is attained within clear limits,

QUESTION

Do you agree with Eliot's idea that individual character is, in crucial ways, determined by social context?

QUESTION

The Brooke sisters lost their parents when they were very young. Do you find that sad fact to be reflected in their individual characters or in the relationship between them?

however, and while social Reform is the big topic of the day, she settles for the stability of a conservative life.

DOROTHEA BROOKE

A young woman of unusual beauty, Dorothea dresses with Puritanic plainness to indicate that she is free from personal vanity (see **Themes: Religion and scepticism**). Yet there is a kind of pride in her aspiration to be more than a feminine adornment, and to help shape the world. Her sister Celia calls her Dodo, with obvious affection, but Dorothea's ardent seriousness often unsettles those who meet her. Celia regards her with 'a mixture of criticism and awe' (p. 15).

Dorothea's idealism seems out of place in provincial England where, in the early 1830s, the materialistic values of the commercial middle class were becoming increasingly influential. She wishes to channel her religious passion into plans for social improvement. She has started an infant school in the village, and her cherished project is to build cottages for local labourers. As a woman, however, there are clear limits to what she can achieve in this patriarchal society, and she is dependent upon the capacity of men to act.

In her marriage to Casaubon an inclination to self-sacrifice is marked; she is filled with 'hopeful dreams, admiring trust, and passionate self-devotion' (p. 71). Such subordination seems inescapable for an intelligent woman in a society designed to promote masculine values. She is heiress to Tipton Grange only in the sense that her son inherits it on her uncle's demise. She has no personal entitlement.

Her friends compare her intelligence unfavourably with her sister's common sense. Dorothea's cleverness does not prevent her making serious errors of judgement, notably in her willingness to marry Casaubon. She consistently looks beyond the requirements of day-to-day living. Celia remarks, 'You always see what nobody else sees; it is impossible to satisfy you; yet you never see what is quite plain. That's your way Dodo' (p. 36). Her intensity produces practical problems, but George Eliot suggests that such vision, often at personal expense, is necessary for the gradual improvement of human society.

At the end of *Middlemarch*, Dorothea marries Will Ladislaw and becomes a wife and mother, although she is still actively philanthropic. Feminist critics have seen this move into contented domesticity as unacceptable capitulation to patriarchal demands. But the compromise shows her acknowledging her own emotional needs as a human being. Her determination to act for herself, very evident at the end of the novel, is an important step away from childlike dependency towards self-fulfilment, in the face of society's disapproval.

MR BULSTRODE

Nicholas Bulstrode the banker is an outsider, 'altogether of dimly known origin' (p. 96), who married Mr Vincy's sister. His speech is fluent and subdued. He is around sixty years old, has 'pale blond skin, thin grey-besprinkled brown hair, light-grey eyes and a large forehead' (p. 123). A respected professional man and philanthropist, pious in religion, he is eventually exposed as a hypocrite and ruthless opportunist, who serves only his self-interest.

He has considerable social power, stemming largely from his control of personal loans and charitable allocations. But he acted unscrupulously in the past and concealment has become 'the habit of his life' (p. 824). The past returns to haunt him in the figure of John Raffles, who extorts money from him. He fears he will become 'an object of scorn and an opprobrium of the religion with which he had diligently associated himself' (p. 615). He is eventually driven by disgrace to leave Middlemarch.

ELINOR CADWALLADER

The wife of the rector of Tipton and Freshitt is 'a lady of immeasurably high birth' (p. 53), a member of the De Bracy family. She belongs to the old aristocracy, but is happily married to a man from a lower social class. Nonetheless, she is an inveterate snob. Her pedigree gives her confidence to speak in a forthright manner, and she injects a note of caustic humour into her comments on Middlemarch life.

 QUESTION

What does George Eliot's depiction of various married couples in *Middlemarch* tell us about the nature of marriage?

HUMPHREY CADWALLADER

The rector of Tipton and Freshitt is 'a large man, with full lips and a sweet smile; very plain and rough in his exterior, but with that solid imperturbable ease and good-humour which is infectious' (p. 68). He is a tolerant man, free from egotism and contented with an unassuming rural existence. For a clergyman he shows remarkably little interest in theology, but is devoted to fishing.

EDWARD CASAUBON

Casaubon, who has lived in Lowick Manor for ten years, is a fairly wealthy man, around forty-five years old, and is Dorothea's first husband. He looks older than his years, with iron-grey hair, deep eye-sockets, spare form, and pale complexion. His eyesight is beginning to fade. Dorothea, in her blinkered idealism, compares him to the philosophers Locke and Pascal, and the poet Milton. Others see him more clearly. Chettam calls him 'a dried bookworm' (p. 22). Mrs Cadwallader calls him 'a great bladder for dried peas to rattle in' (p. 58), and jokes that when a drop of his blood was placed under a microscope 'it was all semi-colons and parentheses' (p. 71). Brooke thinks he is destined to be a bishop, but Casaubon dies of a heart-attack, after a life of futile labour and unreflecting egotism.

The scholarly Casaubon inhabits a world of knowledge from which Dorothea, as a woman, has been excluded, and to which she craves entry. This is the basis for their marriage. Her narrow education, described as a 'toy-box history of the world' (p. 86), combines with her ardent imagination to envisage this world as a place of wonders. She is totally devoted to her husband's grand project, seeking to uncover the key to all mythologies. Casaubon has moments of despondency, 'toiling in the morass of authorship without seeming nearer to the goal' (p. 85). But it is Casaubon's cousin, Will Ladislaw, who discloses to Dorothea that the scholar's ignorance of German has left him unaware of work that renders his own obsolete.

SIR JAMES CHETTAM

Chettam is a handsome baronet, a 'blooming Englishman of the red-whiskered type' (p. 16). He is described as amiable and he

? QUESTION

Casaubon is a dry, lifeless scholar. But George Eliot was a fiercely intellectual woman, who had read a great deal and engaged actively in critical debates of her day. What does *Middlemarch* tell us about intellectual pursuits?

knows the limits of his abilities, so he and Celia Brooke are obviously compatible. Initially, he hopes to marry Dorothea, but being a man who cares little for ideas he does not meet her demands. He does implement her plan for cottages on his estate, however, even after the marriage to Casaubon. This may indicate his continuing admiration for her; certainly, he shows concern for her and is outraged at both her marriages. But Chettam seems genuinely altruistic; he is highly critical of Brooke's lapses in caring for his tenants. A less charitable interpretation might suggest that, in a period of agitation for Reform, it is politically advantageous for a member of the aristocracy to avoid discontent amongst his own tenants.

CAMDEN FAREBROTHER

Farebrother's physical appearance is vividly described in the novel (see **Characterisation**). He is an affable and outgoing clergyman, whose passion is the study of Natural History. This interest helps him establish a sympathetic relationship with Lydgate. His preaching is 'ingenious and pithy' (p. 178), delivered without a book, and it draws a good congregation. He lives with his mother, sister, and aunt. Farebrother is in love with Mary Garth, but stands aside to enable Fred Vincy to marry her.

PETER FEATHERSTONE

Featherstone is a wealthy old invalid, whose second wife was Mrs Vincy's sister. Fred Vincy regularly visits him at Stone Court, anticipating a substantial legacy, as the old man is thought to be childless. But it transpires that Featherstone has an illegitimate son, Joshua Rigg, who inherits the estate.

The old man derives sadistic pleasure from humiliating Fred. He also enjoys being cruel to Mary Garth, whom he employs to look after him: 'It was usual with him to season his pleasure in showing favour to one person by being especially disagreeable to another, and Mary was always at hand to furnish the condiment' (p. 133). He stops her reading while she sits with him. In his stridently patriarchal view 'Home Sweet Home' is 'the suitable garnish for girls' (p. 116).

CHECK THE BOOK

Before botany and zoology became the province of specialists there was a popular fashion for Natural History. In nineteenth century Britain amateur clubs were formed for adults and children to observe and learn about all kinds of native wildlife, including fossils. Clergymen played a prominent role in organising such clubs and adding to knowledge about Natural History topics. David Elliston Allen has written *The Naturalist in Britain* (Pelican Books, 1978), a social history of the subject.

CALEB AND SUSAN GARTH

Caleb Garth, Mary's father, is a kindly surveyor, valuer, and land-
agent. He is a man of great integrity and honesty, who refuses to
participate in any activity which might be considered disreputable.
His practical knowledge is widely recognised, and he is sought after
as a farm manager. He reveres work and has a passion for
machinery, but he pays little heed to money, and at the start of the
novel he is still reeling from the failure of his building business. He
is a rounded man, who wants his son Alfred to become an engineer,
but also loves music. Importantly, he respects his wife, and
invariably consults with her before arriving at any significant
decision.

Susan Garth was a teacher before she married Caleb. She is 'the
same curly haired square-faced type as Mary, but handsomer, with
more delicacy of feature, a pale skin, a solid matronly figure, and a
remarkable firmness of glance' (p. 244). She has four sons and two
daughters. She is generous and intelligent, but adheres to the belief
that women should subordinate their interests to those of men.

MARY GARTH

QUESTION

Mary attracts two
very different
types of suitor in
Fred and Mr
Farebrother. What
does this say about
her character?

Mary is small and broad featured, with brown curly hair. Her
plainness is accentuated when she is in the company of Rosamond
Vincy, who regards her as 'sensible and useful' (p. 113). Unlike
Rosamond she has a pronounced sense of ironic humour. She tends
to talk in generalities rather than speaking of particular cases,
drawing broad lessons from specific experiences, rather than
indulging in gossip. She is a character who sees things plainly, largely
due to her remarkable capacity for detachment, and she reports
what she sees with frank honesty. She has no ambition to change the
world, but her practicality and sympathetic nature create the
conditions for friendly social relationships and a happy marriage.

WILL LADISLAW

The grandson of Casaubon's aunt Julia, Ladislaw has inherited her
grey eyes, quite close together. He has light brown curls, and a
'delicate irregular nose with a little ripple in it' (p. 79). He was
educated at Rugby School and the University of Heidelberg, but has

not settled to a career. Rather, he travels across Europe, studying art, and other manifestations of the poetic imagination.

The contrast to his scholarly cousin could not be more dramatic. Ladislaw is compared to the dashing **Romantic** poets Shelley and Byron. He writes poetry, sings, and draws pictures. He declares that his religion is 'to love what is good and beautiful when I see it' (p. 392). He has a lively sense of humour, is fond of children, and befriends Farebrother's eccentric aunt, Miss Noble. He aims to conduct himself with honour and integrity, but his passionate and spontaneously rebellious nature at times results in unruly behaviour and inconsiderate outbursts.

He becomes Dorothea's second husband, and is elected as a reforming Member of Parliament, yet since the novel's publication there have been critics who have protested that Ladislaw is too lightweight to bear the significance allocated to him. They have detected a lack of adequate realism in George Eliot's portrayal of a figure who 'looked like an incarnation of the spring whose spirit filled the air – a bright creature, abundant in uncertain promises' (p. 471). It has been suggested that he serves primarily to heighten our sense of Dorothea's real worth, after the folly of her marriage to Casaubon.

TERTIUS LYDGATE

Lydgate has 'heavy eyebrows, dark eyes, a straight nose, thick dark hair, large solid white hands' (p. 114). There is 'a certain careless refinement about his toilette and utterance' (p. 92). His voice is 'deep and sonorous' (p. 125). After studying medicine in London, Edinburgh, and Paris he arrives in Middlemarch, aged twenty-seven, and assumes responsibility for supervision of the new hospital. He introduces new medical practices, and is passionately concerned for reform of his profession, and for innovative research.

His idealism and 'intellectual passion' (p. 144) disclose an affinity with Dorothea. Like her, he is reputedly 'very clever' (p. 91), and he is keen to help others, especially the poor. He has chosen a profession that requires 'the highest intellectual strain' while keeping him 'in good warm contact with his neighbours' (p. 165).

CONTEXT

Medical study was expensive during the early and mid nineteenth century. Lydgate was able attend major medical schools because of his family's wealth. The 1858 Medical Act brought about long overdue regulation of the qualifications of medical practitioners; at the time Lydgate was practising the British medical profession was very variable in terms of training, knowledge, and ability.

CHECK THE BOOK

Father and Son (1907) is a memoir by Edmund Gosse (1849–1928) which tells how Darwin's theory of evolution had a hugely unsettling impact upon Gosse's own father, a devout Christian, but also a keen, largely self-taught zoologist and student of marine biology. *Father and Son* registers a significant historical shift from amateur science based in close and careful observation to a far more specialised and theoretically sophisticated kind of scientific understanding.

He regards science as 'the inward light which is the last refinement of Energy, capable of bathing even the ethereal atoms in its ideally illuminated space' (pp. 164–5). But his quest for a primitive tissue from which all others are derived is destined, like Casaubon's search for the key to mythologies, to end in failure.

The name Tertius indicates that he is a third son, and so is disadvantaged in terms of inheritance, even though he is well connected, being related to the aristocratic Lydgates of Northumberland. He is determined to make his own way in the world, and enters his profession with zeal, but money troubles increasingly compromise his lofty aspirations. He is contemptuous of pettiness and ignorance, but his arrogance prevents him addressing them directly, in order to overcome them.

During his time in Paris he was passionately infatuated with an actress who killed her husband. This was an uncharacteristic lapse of self-control for a man whom Fred Vincy calls 'a prig' (p. 158). Lydgate's father was a military man, although, like Dorothea, he was orphaned early. On his own request, his guardians apprenticed him to a country medical practitioner.

His marriage to Rosamond is as debilitating as Dorothea's marriage to Casaubon. They inhabit separate worlds of understanding and have no interests in common. He sees his wife through a lens of deeply ingrained patriarchal assumptions. He 'was no radical in relation to anything but medical reform and the prosecution of discovery. In the rest of practical life he walked by hereditary habit' (pp. 348–9). After leaving Middlemarch he becomes a successful practitioner in London before dying at fifty.

JOHN RAFFLES

Approaching sixty, Rigg's stepfather John Raffles is 'very florid and hairy, with much grey in his bushy whiskers and thick curly hair'. He is stout and has 'the air of a swaggerer' (p. 413). He has spent ten years in America supported by money from Bulstrode. He now seeks to extort more money, threatening to expose the banker's sordid past. He becomes very ill due to alcoholic poisoning, and dies at Stone Court, while in Bulstrode's care.

JOSHUA RIGG

Rigg is Featherstone's illegitimate son, now in his early thirties. He has bulging eyes, a 'thin-lipped, downward-curved mouth, and hair sleekly brushed away from a forehead that sank suddenly above the ridge of the eyebrows' (p. 332). He is 'sleek, neat, and cool' like the frog he resembles (p. 413), and has 'a high chirping voice' (p. 340). He has worked as a clerk and accountant in a small commercial business in a seaport. After selling Stone Court to Bulstrode, he achieves his materialistic ambition of becoming a money-changer in a busy port.

FRED VINCY

Rosamond's brother Fred is good-natured, but is recognised as 'the family laggard' (p. 97). He is evidently unsuited for business. Fred's idleness is in part due to his expectation that he will receive a substantial legacy from Peter Featherstone. That expectation is disappointed. Mr Vincy wishes him to train for the clergy, and Fred eventually completes his degree. However, he lacks the vocation, and is pleased to be apprenticed to Caleb Garth as a farm manager. He eventually becomes a successful farmer. His love for Mary Garth remains unwavering through the financially troubled phase of his life, and is rewarded with a happy marriage to her.

ROSAMOND VINCY

The beauty of Mr Vincy's daughter Rosamond, a graceful, blue-eyed blonde, is widely admired by the men of Middlemarch. In consequence:

> every nerve and muscle in Rosamond was adjusted to the consciousness that she was being looked at. She was by nature an actress of parts that entered into her *physique*: she even acted her own character, and so well, that she did not know it to be precisely her own. (p. 117)

Her education has trained her to be ladylike, with an emphasis on feminine elegance, and an avoidance of weighty matters. She is a fluent pianist. Lydgate is attracted to her as a decorative adornment, but she is strong willed, and her obsession with social rank and material advancement places their marriage under considerable strain.

CHECK THE BOOK
An essay in John Sutherland's stimulating *Is Heathcliff a Murderer?: Great puzzles in nineteenth-century fiction* (Oxford University Press, 2005; 1996) poses the question as to whether Will Ladislaw was illegitimate.

QUESTION

Do you think George Eliot has conformed to a stereotype in her characterisation of Rosamond Vincy?

It is tempting to see Rosamond as a shallow egotist, but Lydgate's sense that 'in poor Rosamond's mind there was not room enough for luxuries to look small in' (p. 701) is unfair. Rosamond is 'clever with that sort of cleverness which catches every tone except the humorous' (p. 159). She is too self-conscious to make jokes, and that self-consciousness is the product of her narrow education and of her upbringing by well meaning but socially ambitious parents.

Dorothea is dazzled by the prospect of a hidden world of knowledge. Rosamond is beguiled by the lifestyle of the upper classes, which lies beyond the social horizon of her middle class manufacturing family. Lydgate attracts her because he comes from beyond that horizon, and evokes 'vistas of that middle-class heaven, rank' (p. 118). Her mother's disparaging remarks about the Garth family indicate that Rosamond has been trained to aspire to 'that celestial condition on earth in which she would have nothing to do with vulgar people' (p. 166). She is undoubtedly selfish, but it is not simply a personal failing.

WALTER AND LUCY VINCY

Walter Vincy, mayor of Middlemarch, is a florid and fleshy man, who has made money from his manufacturing business. He is a respectable figure, but spends his days at the warehouse, and belongs to a different social class to the inhabitants of Tipton Grange and Freshitt Hall. He has 'expensive Middlemarch habits', spending money on coursing, his cellar, and dinner parties (p. 230). His sister, Harriet, is married to Nicholas Bulstrode.

His wife Lucy, forty-five years old, radiates good humour. She was an innkeeper's daughter, and has a 'tinge of unpretentious, inoffensive vulgarity' (p. 158). She appears snobbish, however, when suggestion arises that Mary Garth may marry her son Fred. Mrs Vincy's sister was the second wife of the wealthy Peter Featherstone.

THEMES

ALTRUISM AND EGOTISM

Characterisation in *Middlemarch* is conceived between the poles of altruism and egotism. Characters change, but each may be measured at any point in the story against a scale that ranges from selfless concern for the well-being of others, to obsessive self-interest. George Eliot undoubtedly expected her readers to consider altruistic behaviour preferable to self-centredness.

The flaws of the novel's evident egotists (such as Casaubon, Bulstrode, and Rosamond Vincy) are clear enough. The **narrator** remarks: 'Will not a tiny speck very close to our vision blot out the glory of the world, and leave only a margin by which we see the blot? I know no speck so troublesome as self' (p. 419). But the altruists also have their failings. Dorothea initially appears haughty and naive in her idealistic outlook. Lydgate's determination to advance the medical profession makes him lamentably inconsiderate at home. Caleb Garth helps others without demanding payment, but as a result his business collapses and his family faces financial difficulty.

The problem is that what is good for one person may have harmful effects upon others. This is compounded by the distortions, which, as the narrator observes, enter into one person's interpretation of another's wishes:

> But how little we know what would make paradise for our neighbours! We judge from our own desires, and our neighbours themselves are not always open enough even to throw out a hint of theirs. (p. 520)

In the short term acts of selfish egotism exert powerful influence upon the course of events. Nonetheless, George Eliot recognised that practical acts of altruism, such as Dorothea's plans to build cottages, Lydgate's concern to improve the medical profession, and Ladislaw's career as a reforming politician, all contribute in some small way to the gradual improvement of human society.

 CHECK THE BOOK

George Eliot's contemporary George Meredith (1828–1909) cast a critical eye upon egotism in the self-absorbed character Sir Willoughby Patterne in *The Egoist* (1879) (Penguin Books, 2007).

THE WEB OF SOCIAL RELATIONSHIPS

There are a number of characters in *Middlemarch* who aspire to control the course of their own lives. They are invariably frustrated in their aspiration. A major theme of the novel is that social relationships form a web that produces interdependence among the characters. No action takes place in isolation; consequences are often unforeseen.

The web provides a structural principle for relationships between various parts of the story. In thematic terms it emphasises limits upon the capacity of individuals to determine their own destiny. As the lives of individuals are inextricably bound to the actions and attitudes of others, a capacity for sympathy is vital. This does not merely involve feeling sorry for others, but necessitates an ability to conceive how life might appear from another's point of view. Throughout *Middlemarch*, Dorothea struggles to achieve such sympathetic understanding.

At the end of the novel, Dorothea has become Mrs Ladislaw, a wife and mother, performing small philanthropic acts. George Eliot seems to suggest that this circumscribed role, falling so far short of Dorothea's earlier ambitions, is the best she can hope for. In a modern democratic society it is not individual heroism, but reforming Acts of Parliament and technological change, such as the advent of the railway, which shape the world in obvious ways. The impact of personal kindness is far less visible, although in the long term it may prove equally important.

In this novel, the individual appears diminished in importance, and that has unsettled some readers, but George Eliot believed that small acts of personal generosity play their part in a gradual evolution towards social improvement. So, in the web of social relationships, each human being should be seen as 'the slow creation of long interchanging influences' (p. 409).

RELIGION AND SCEPTICISM

In George Eliot's day, the aristocracy and landed gentry, such as Chettam and Brooke, mostly belonged to the Church of England.

QUESTION

Where in *Middlemarch* do you detect genuine capacity for sympathy and sympathetic action amongst the characters?

QUESTION

Does the web of social relationships also have negative effects on characters, specifically in terms of gossip and scandal?

Many of those engaged in commerce were dissenting Protestants. It is a measure of Bulstrode's acquired social power, as well as of his hypocrisy, that after many years as a committed non-conformist, he has changed his allegiance to the established Anglican church. Note that Brooke had an ancestor who was 'a Puritan gentleman who served under Cromwell, but afterwards conformed, and managed to come out of all political troubles as the proprietor of a respectable family estate' (p. 7).

Dorothea belongs to the Anglican establishment, and she marries a clergyman, yet she 'had been brought up in English and Swiss Puritanism, fed on meagre Protestant histories' (p. 193). Non-conformity is manifested in her determined individualism; she follows her own conscience, rather than being circumscribed by the accepted view. She speaks of her own flexibility in religion:

> whenever I find one way that makes it a wider blessing than any other, I cling to that as the truest – I mean that which takes in the most good of all kinds, and brings in the most people as sharers in it. (p. 495)

Extending this liberal point of view, the **narrator** refers disparagingly to low church intolerance of any form of sensual indulgence:

> The Vincys had the readiness to enjoy, the rejection of all anxiety, and the belief in life as a merry lot, which made a house exceptional in most county towns at that time, when Evangelicalism had cast a certain suspicion as of a plague-infection over the few amusements which had survived in the provinces. (p. 161)

Such observations also feed into the novel a sense of the historical realities of the period.

Importantly, George Eliot shows Christianity to be a belief that encompasses divergent points of view, rather than being the monolithic authority it had been during the European middle ages. The existence of variant interpretations in all fields of human understanding is one of the major thematic concerns in *Middlemarch*. Reference to reforms extending rights to

CONTEXT

The established Christian Church in England follows a tradition of faith known as Anglicanism, which occupies the middle ground between Roman Catholicism and Protestantism. Non-Anglican Christians, who do not accept the beliefs and practices of the established Church, are known in the United Kingdom as non-conformists. The term non-conformism includes groups such as the Methodists, Baptists, Unitarians, and Quakers.

CONTEXT

Strict adherents to Anglican faith are sometimes called 'high church'; those who favour more liberal or dissenting views and practices are sometimes called 'low church'.

CHECK THE BOOK

Charles Darwin's *On the Origin of Species by Means of Natural Selection* (1859) (Penguin Books, 1982) had an enormous impact on the thinking and the faith of late Victorian intellectuals.

non-Anglicans also reflects the novel's concern with the possibility of social change (see Chapter 1 and 'the Catholic Question', p. 9). If reform in terms of both class and religion could occur, then modification of the status of women was also conceivable.

Despite the progressive attitudes to religion in the novel, and the scepticism of its author, faith is still an important part of the social model it advocates. The **narrator** of *Middlemarch* observes that 'scepticism, as we know, can never be thoroughly applied, else life would come to a standstill: something we must believe in and do' (p. 240). Dorothea's belief is:

> That by desiring what is perfectly good, even when we don't quite know what it is and cannot do what we would, we are part of the divine power against evil – widening the skirts of light and making the struggle with darkness narrower. (p. 392)

George Eliot herself appears to have espoused a secular version of this faith.

The evolutionary theory of Charles Darwin (1809–82) fuelled what Hutton called the 'great wave of scepticism', as it appeared to discredit the Biblical account of Creation. But making a positive variation on Darwinian theory, *Middlemarch* suggests that although individuals may fail to meet their aspirations, the gradual evolution of human society is served by that personal vision which does not merely settle for the way things are in the present. What remained unsettling for many of Eliot's contemporaries, however, was the diminished role the individual life seemed to play within this evolutionary process.

SOCIAL CLASS

The historical dimension of *Middlemarch*, set forty years before its actual composition, draws attention to processes of social change. In English society such change has invariably led to changes in the relationship between social classes.

George Eliot portrays English society across the class spectrum, from the aristocratic Mrs Cadwallader and the baronet Sir James Chettam, through members of the gentry such as Brooke and

Casaubon, the successful, commercial middle class, such as
Bulstrode and the Vincys, the lower middle class Garth family, and
working class characters such as Dagley and Mrs Dollop.

Mrs Cadwallader's capacity for upper class snobbery is evident,
although usually softened with **irony**, as when she says to Celia,
'Young people should think of their families in marrying. I set a bad
example – married a poor clergyman, and made myself a pitiable
object among the De Bracys' (p. 56). Snobbishness is also present in
Sir Godwin Lydgate's letter, where he announces to his nephew,
'I have nothing to do with men of your profession' (p. 664).

QUESTION

Does the **narrator**
reveal an affinity
with any particular
class?

The aptly named inn landlady Mrs Dollop is at the other extreme of
the social scale to Sir Godwin but, in her own way, she concurs in
her evaluation of the medical profession: 'I know what doctors are.
They're a deal too cunning to be found out' (p.723). Snobbery
permeates down through the ranks of social status. Mr Dill, the
barber, 'felt himself a little above his company at Dollop's, but liked
it none the worse' (p. 722).

But it is a society in transition. Science and professionalism are
socially ascendant. Even the kind of influence which accrues, for
better or worse, to a man such as Bulstrode is an indication of a
changing structure of social power, and the influence of 'new
money'.

MONEY, INCOME, AND DEBT

References in *Middlemarch* to tithes, the age-old practice of
payment by means of actual physical produce, may remind us that
money is, essentially, an abstract system of exchange; coins or
banknotes are tokens of their equivalent value in physical goods or
services. Yet money exerts a very real, physical, and immediate
influence upon characters in the novel, as in life.

Money courses through the veins of communal life in Middlemarch.
It surfaces at auctions and horse-fairs, in the threat of bankruptcy
and in hopes of inheritance, in terms of earning power, debt,
gambling, philanthropic funding, fraud, and regular commerce. It
affects almost all the characters in the novel, but most powerfully

MONEY, INCOME, AND DEBT continued

Fred Vincy and Tertius Lydgate who are both touched by debt. Money is prized by the middle classes as a means to acquire greater social status and power, and it is valued by idealists for its capacity to transform the lives of the poor, sick, and needy.

Joshua Rigg appears as if from nowhere, collects his inheritance and then moves on to a busy port where he can live out his dream of being a money-changer. The farmers who for centuries paid tithes in the vicinity of Middlemarch are rooted to the land and regulated by the seasons. They are fixed in place by their work. Rigg is a creature of money; he is consequently mobile and lives where currencies flow rather than where crops grow. *Middlemarch* is in this way vitally concerned with social change. The fluidity of money as a medium of exchange and as an agent of social change makes it a key thematic ingredient.

THE ROLE OF WOMEN

George Eliot was cautious in her view of the need for change in gender relationships. She always favoured gradual evolution over militant clamour. But Dorothea and Rosamond clearly suffer on account of the limits imposed on their view of the world by their upbringing and their education.

CHECK THE BOOK

Middlemarch portrays a patriarchal society, that is, one in which conventionally masculine values are dominant. That dominance had been challenged by writers such as Mary Wollstonecraft, in her *Vindication of the Rights of Woman* (1792) (Penguin Books, 2004) and by John Stuart Mill in *The Subjection of Women* (1869) (Penguin Books, 2003).

Patriarchal assumptions are evident in Chettam's conviction that masculinity is in itself an advantage. Men are superior to women, he believes, 'as the smallest birch-tree is of a higher kind than the most soaring palm' (p. 21). Arthur Brooke's condescending view of Dorothea's aspirations is manifested in a series of patronising remarks, such as, 'We must not have you getting too learned for a woman, you know' (p. 338), and 'deep studies, classics, mathematics, that kind of thing, are too taxing for a woman' (p. 65).

In an essay called 'Silly Novels by Lady Novelists', written for the *Westminster Review* in 1856, George Eliot criticised lightweight fiction written by women, because it tended to fuel prejudice against 'the more solid education of women'. Lack of solid education proves a damaging obstacle in Dorothea's and Rosamond's relationships with their husbands. Lydgate wants his wife to be docile. He distrusts clever women, such as Dorothea:

> It is troublesome to talk to such women. They are always wanting reasons, yet they are too ignorant to understand the merits of any question, and usually fall back on their moral sense to settle things after their own taste. (p. 93)

For much of the nineteenth century, daughters received little formal education, unless their parents had sufficient wealth to pay for special tutelage. Even then, the quality of the experience was markedly lower than for their male counterparts. Social accomplishments such as playing the piano, 'a small kind of tinkling which symbolized the aesthetic part of the young ladies' education' (p. 45), were considered a more fitting training than intellectually challenging subjects. George Eliot felt that women should have equal access to basic knowledge. She refused to be dogmatic, however; education should meet different needs.

Fred Vincy goes through the motions of taking his degree at university, but his temperament befits him for practical work. Mary Garth, who has been bullied by Peter Featherstone, and prevented from reading in his company, eventually writes a book. But she was raised by a mother who viewed the subordination of women to men as proper, and significantly Mary's book is not a feminist tract but relates stories of great men.

Some of George Eliot's close friends, such as Barbara Bodichon, sought reforms in the spheres of law, politics, and education. Eliot harboured suspicions that such reforms would impair women's capacity for compassionate action. She felt that women have a capacity for empathy which is often missing from patriarchal conduct, and wished to promote this quality, but remained unsure how best that might be done.

LOCATION AND THE IMPORTANCE OF PLACE

In a sense Middlemarch is a representative location – a growing and prospering town, surrounded by countryside and villages, in the English Midlands during a period of distinct transition. Within its landscape buildings enshrine the past – the names Manor, Court, and Grange refer back to a medieval society ordered along feudal and monastic lines, a world that that has been superseded by an

CHECK THE BOOK
'Silly Novels by Lady Novelists' is republished in George Eliot, *Selected Critical Writings* (Oxford University Press, 1992) and in *Selected Essays, Poems and Other Writings* (Penguin Books, 1990).

**CHECK
THE BOOK**
George Eliot's older contemporary Elizabeth Gaskell (1810–65) was born in London but moved while still young to Knutsford in Cheshire, which she used as the basis for her gentle novel *Cranford* (1851). Drawing attention to the dramatic contrasts between England's industrial North and more affluent South she used Victorian Manchester as the basis for setting her more powerful novel *North and South* (1855).

industrialised capitalist economy and an increasingly democratic social order. George Eliot manages, however, to create a strong sense of a particular place, in which are imbedded the lives of her vividly drawn characters.

Caleb Garth's house is described as 'a homely place with an orchard in front of it, a rambling, old-fashioned, halftimbered building, which before the town had spread had been a farmhouse, but was now surrounded with the private gardens of the townsmen' (p. 242). In this brief delineation, George Eliot conveys the setting, the character of the Garth family – who fit very well into their immediate surroundings – and also a sense of broad historical change as the town encroaches upon the farm, and individual members of the prospering middle class assert themselves through their new homes. The balance of the economy is steadily changing from agriculture to industry, and power is gradually passing from the old landowners to the new commercial class, who make their money not from local fields but from trade with distant places.

The subtitle of *Middlemarch* is 'A Study of Provincial Life'. During the nineteenth century there were significant changes in the relationship between London, as the nation's capital city, and outlying provinces. Daily life for individuals throughout Britain became increasingly influenced by decisions taken in Parliament. Electoral reform enfranchised many more adult males. The extension of the right to participate in a modern democracy corresponded to an increasing degree of regulation extending from the metropolitan centre.

A highly significant intervention of this kind was the Elementary Education Act, passed in 1870, just before *Middlemarch* was published. Although it empowered individuals by ensuring basic literacy and numeracy for all, it also drew children across Britain into a standardised system of learning. *Middlemarch* is, in part, about this process of change during a slightly earlier yet crucial phase of British history. The benefits of reform are to be weighed against disruption to traditional ways of living and working.

During the mid nineteenth century towns often became crowded and insanitary as unemployed rural workers moved away from the land in search of jobs in the new and expanding industrial centres. In *Middlemarch*, the names of Slaughter Lane and its landlady Mrs Dollop effectively evoke the negative side of town life (see Chapters 45 and 71). They contrast starkly with the narrator's evocation of a 'delightful morning when the hayricks at Stone Court were scenting the air quite impartially' (p. 535), or the contented Garth family group 'dogs and cats included, under the great apple-tree in the orchard' (p. 571).

In her introductory chapter to *Felix Holt* (1866), George Eliot had emphatically registered her sense of good things lost in the process of historical change. Nonetheless, despite her perception that a certain form of communal life had largely been lost, and with it a particular sensibility, she suggests in *Middlemarch* that social and political reform eventually bring about beneficial changes.

LANGUAGE AND STYLE

GEORGE ELIOT'S LITERARY REALISM

George Eliot's early work displays her commitment to a fairly straightforward conception of **realism**, in which the writer's obligation is to produce an accurate representation of the known world, a faithful reflection of people and the way they live.

By the time she wrote *Middlemarch*, matters had become more complex. She still aspired to represent the known world, but she recognised that knowledge itself had become fraught with problems. This was especially the case since she had lost the certainties of youthful religious zeal, and she saw that many other intellectuals had similarly lost faith in orthodox Christianity.

In *Middlemarch*, shared understanding has evidently been displaced by conflicting interpretations. Casaubon's work has been superseded by new theories offered by German scholars. Lydgate finds himself at odds with older doctors over his innovative methods and attitudes. On a more mundane level, local labourers

 **CHECK THE BOOK**

In Thomas Hardy's *Tess of the d'Urbervilles* (1891) (Penguin Books, 2003) local distinctness is significantly eroded by metropolitan influence. A schoolteacher from London, working at a village school in Wessex, trains Tess Durbeyfield to speak English very differently from her mother's usage. Hardy's novel also registers the impact of the railway, connecting isolated villages to the capital city, collapsing the distance between them.

view the railway as a dangerous presence in their locality, while Caleb Garth seeks to assure them of its benefits.

A customary requirement of literary **realism** is that neither language nor style should obtrude. A priority of this kind of writing is to enable readers to feel that they know the characters and communities depicted. If language and style lose their transparency they distract attention from the story and complicate our sense of understanding. George Eliot introduces humour into her novel with the character Borthrop Trumbull, 'an amateur of superior phrases' (p. 310), who relishes words for their own sake and consequently appears rather foolish.

Middlemarch is primarily a realist novel, but it is concerned with the complexities of psychological states, and was written with a late nineteenth century awareness that knowledge, in science and philosophy, had become provisional and unstable. So although language is approached foremost as a vehicle for the story, George Eliot also directs us to the fact that words are used in differing ways in different contexts. This suggests that no single way of speaking about the world is adequate to understand it completely.

EPIGRAPHS

The **epigraphs** that head each chapter reflect the changing nature of the English language, from Geoffrey Chaucer (*c.* 1343–1400) through to George Eliot's own invented quotations. There are also quotations in Spanish, French, and Italian. We may recall that it is Casaubon's ignorance of German that blinds him to the limitations of his own work.

VOCABULARY

Fred Vincy criticises poets who persist in archaic usages inappropriate to their time, calling an ox 'a *leg-plaiter*' (p. 99). That antiquated term referred to the way oxen walked, crossing their legs with each step. It is picturesque, but old-fashioned. George Eliot's vocabulary, on the other hand, as the narrator, is appropriate to life in an England where the railway had arrived and industrial towns and cities thrived.

CONTEXT

The novelist Henry James (1843–1916) suggested, in *Galaxy* magazine in 1873, that *Middlemarch* sets a limit to 'the development of the old-fashioned English novel'. Simple realism, based on a common sense of knowing the world, no longer seemed viable.

She introduces words from contemporary science, conveying a sense of the age, and bolstering characterisation of the doctor, Lydgate, and of Farebrother who has a passion for Natural History. Such words also indicate that a specialised vocabulary contributes to a different model of understanding. For example, Farebrother refers to 'orthoptera' (p. 172) – the order of insects that includes grasshoppers. He also refers to a recently published book entitled *Microscopic Observations on the Pollen of Plants* (p. 173). Microscopes have been made since around 1600, but their manufacture became much more efficient during the nineteenth century and by the time *Middlemarch* was written amateur microscopy had become a quite popular pastime.

Talking with Farebrother, Lydgate thinks: 'A model clergyman, like a model doctor, ought to think his own profession the finest in the world, and take all knowledge as mere nourishment for his moral pathology and therapeutics' (p.176). Nonetheless, medical knowledge leads to a perception of human beings which is very different to that held by theologians, philosophers, painters, or poets.

CHECK THE BOOK
A sophisticated look at George Eliot's use of scientific language and its connection to her presentation of religious issues can be found in Michael Davis's *George Eliot and Nineteenth-Century Psychology* (Ashgate Publishing, 2006).

DIALECT

George Eliot includes some **dialect**, representing the manner of speaking particular to the Middlemarch area. Fred Vincy says to Rosamond that 'All choice of words is slang. It marks a class' (p. 99). Local dialect in *Middlemarch* marks the working class characters, such as Dagley in Chapter 39, or the labourers in Chapter 56. It is indicative of the characters' limited horizons. Their usage is steeped in a traditional way of living, without the education which has steered members of the middle classes towards a standardised way of speaking English. In Chapter 24, Mrs Garth endeavours to teach her youngest children 'to speak and write correctly, so that you can be understood', unlike old Job, the labourer whose quaint way of speaking seems to belong to an earlier age (p. 244).

METAPHORS

In Chapter 10, the narrator observes that 'we all of us, grave or light, get our thoughts entangled in metaphors, and act fatally on

**CHECK
THE BOOK**
In *Middlemarch* George Eliot addresses the aspirations of a sensitive and intelligent woman in provincial England. In France, far more controversially, the novel *Madame Bovary* (1856) by Gustave Flaubert (1821–80) depicted a woman reacting against the constraints and tedium of provincial married life by entering into a series of adulterous affairs. Initially prosecuted for its alleged obscenity, *Madame Bovary* is now, like *Middlemarch*, acknowledged as one of the greatest nineteenth-century European novels.

the strength of them' (p. 85). The remark is intended to cast light upon Casaubon's flawed conception of the ways of the world. It refers to a **metaphor** drawn specifically from economics: the scholar's expectation of 'a compound interest of enjoyment' stored up during his years as a bachelor (p. 85). In a novel where Bulstrode, a banker, exercises considerable social influence, and where Lydgate and Fred Vincy are troubled by debts, the metaphor has particular resonance. George Eliot uses metaphors to trace such threads running through this long novel. They allow us to make telling connections.

Images of mirrors and windows are used metaphorically in *Middlemarch* to signal problems arising with regard to knowledge of the self and of its relationship to the world. For example, Lady Chettam reports that her son, James, considers Dorothea to be 'the mirror of all women' (p. 91). Here, the mirror suggests not an accurate reflection but an idealised picture of her. Dorothea's sense of confinement within a sterile marriage is conveyed by the view from the bow-window, which frames 'the still white enclosure which made her visible world' (p. 274). The image of the pier-glass which opens Book Three is a more extended and elaborate metaphor addressing the way in which one's sense of self shapes one's perception of the world.

As the narrator's observation indicates, we use metaphors as an aid to understanding, but they tend to entangle our thoughts and mislead us. Another prominent metaphor that recurs in the book is the labyrinth, suggesting the maze of confused and conflicting impressions and expectations that form a large part of human experience. Characters such as Casaubon and Lydgate, professionally engaged with issues of knowledge, hope to find a thread to lead them through the labyrinth, but none materialises. In Chapter 3, the **narrator** remarks of Dorothea:

> The intensity of her religious disposition, the coercion it exercised over her life, was but one aspect of a nature altogether ardent, theoretic, and intellectually consequent: and with such a nature, struggling in the bands of a narrow teaching, hemmed in by a social life which seemed nothing but a labyrinth of petty

courses, a walled-in maze of small paths that led no whither, the outcome was sure to strike others as at once exaggeration and inconsistency. (pp. 28–9)

Another prominent metaphor, the web, illustrates that threads followed by individual characters only lead to entanglement with the lives of others. Nobody lives in isolation; a social web binds together the fortunes of disparate persons. In the 'Finale' the narrator remarks that 'the fragment of a life, however typical, is not the sample of an even web' (p. 832). Numerous other instances of the web metaphor precede this one, including reference to the French surgeon Bichat's theory that living bodies 'must be regarded as consisting of certain primary webs or tissues' (p. 148).

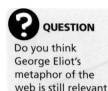

QUESTION

Do you think George Eliot's metaphor of the web is still relevant to today's society?

NARRATIVE TECHNIQUE

STRUCTURE

Middlemarch is divided into eight books, each of which bears a title that hints at the principal concern of that phase of the story. The books are framed by a brief prelude and finale.

George Eliot began with the intention of writing two stories, one entitled 'Miss Brooke', the other depicting life in the provincial town of Middlemarch, with a young doctor as the main character. These separate stories were subsequently fused in the first eighteen chapters of the novel. Out of this fusion the novelist developed an elaborate series of parallels in terms of character, event, and theme, enabling her to bind the various strands of this massive book into close relationships. So, Dorothea's passionate nature is mirrored in Lydgate's intensity; both make unsuitable marriages; and both eventually compromise their idealism.

As already discussed, one of the presiding metaphors of *Middlemarch* is the web. The plot of the novel itself resembles a web. As it unfolds relationships are disclosed connecting apparently separate characters. Will Ladislaw discovers that his grandmother was formerly married to Bulstrode. There are many other less obvious links, and chains of events with unforeseen consequences.

George Eliot recognised that this network of social relationships placed limits upon the capacity of individuals to shape the course of their own lives. This had significant implications for her characterisation of figures such as Dorothea, Lydgate, Casaubon, and Ladislaw, all of whom strive for personal goals which are denied to them by circumstances beyond their control.

These parallels and connections have impressed critics with a sense of the novel's structural integrity. Despite the size of the book, George Eliot leaves no loose ends. She manages to bring together an overview of an historical period and a place, with accounts of the intimate experiences of individual characters, rendered through a series of dramatic scenes. These scenes often involve tense encounters, with characters confronting one another in states of heightened emotion. Often, the scenes involve mistaken interpretations of actions or intentions, which later result in further scenes of similar intensity.

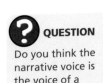

QUESTION

Do you think the narrative voice is the voice of a woman or a man? Is it possible to tell?

NARRATIVE VOICE

The **narrative voice** is a prominent element in *Middlemarch*, steering us through the account of events and shedding light on characters' motives and reactions. It would be naive to regard this voice as a straightforward vehicle for George Eliot's personal views. The author is creating it as a device to complicate and enrich our responses. It can be both critical and sympathetic, and can vary in tone.

Middlemarch follows the example of Henry Fielding (1707–54) in its use of an **omniscient narrator**. The narrative voice in *Middlemarch* is omniscient in the sense that it has access to characters' thoughts, and can report separate events occurring simultaneously, but it always implies the possibility of other points of view. For George Eliot omniscience was compromised by the same scepticism which precluded her belief in an all-knowing God. A significant number of her contemporaries shared this scepticism (see **Themes: Religion and scepticism**).

Chapter 1 starts with the observation, 'Miss Brooke had that kind of beauty which seems to be thrown into relief by poor dress' (p. 7). It is a simple yet surprising declaration; one that is clearly considered, informed by assured notions of beauty, and confident in its judgement, despite use of the conditional word 'seems'. Characterisation of Dorothea is built upon this sentence, which also refers us back directly to the preceding discussion of Saint Theresa. The narrative voice is immediately established as a knowledgeable guide, able to evaluate this young woman in an aesthetic context that soon accommodates reference to the work of Italian painters.

Look at the opening words of Chapter 29: 'One morning, some weeks after her arrival at Lowick, Dorothea – but why always Dorothea? Was her point of view the only possible one with regard to this marriage?' (p. 278). Our reliable guide now seems determined to deprive us of the security of the simple fact, simply told. Instead the world seems open to interpretation in a far more troublesome way. If no single point of view is authoritative then our guide's assertions themselves become provisional. By challenging the priority of Dorothea's point of view the narrative voice in effect calls itself into question.

The **narrator** who registers the small practical details of daily life for this cast of characters – when they make tea, for instance, or play billiards – is also privy to their inner responses, deep feelings, and imaginings. At times we credit this voice with God-like omniscience. But then we are restored to a sense of the relativity of all understanding, as when Chapter 40 begins:

> In watching effects, if only of an electric battery, it is often necessary to change our place and examine a particular mixture or group at some distance from the point where the movement we are interested in was set up. (p. 399)

Suddenly we are in the presence of an empirical scientist, observing an experiment. This narrative voice is slippery but it nonetheless carries us efficiently and fluently through the twists and turns of a very long novel.

THE GENERAL AND THE PARTICULAR

One of the most noticeable characteristics of the narrator is a persistent tendency to draw general conclusions from specific cases.

QUESTION

Virginia Woolf wrote that, 'Those who fall foul of George Eliot do so, we incline to think, on account of her heroines; and with good reason; for there is no doubt that they bring out the worst of her, lead her into difficult places, make her self-conscious, didactic, and occasionally vulgar.' Do you find this a valid criticism with reference to Dorothea Brooke?

We may regard this an aspect of **narratorial omniscience**, although the voice has less in common with an all-knowing God than with a scientist deriving laws from particular observations. The narrator's practice seems to be summed up in Lydgate's remark that the 'mind must be continually expanding and shrinking between the whole human horizon and the horizon of an object-glass' (p. 640).

It may be that in a world where religious and scientific certainties no longer offered consolation and assurance, George Eliot was searching to establish tenable moral principles through generalisation. It has the effect of drawing readers into the frame; we are made to recognise that an apparently localised event may have relevance for us, in our lives.

To counter Henry James's criticism of Eliot's approach, we might note the narrator's observation that, 'There is no general doctrine which is not capable of eating out our morality if unchecked by the deep-seated habit of direct fellow-feeling with individual fellow-men' (p. 619). Sympathetic understanding rather than abstract moral principle is the real requirement. It is an evident failing that Dorothea's 'ardent nature turned all her small allowance of knowledge into principles, fusing her actions in their mould' (p. 193). The important change she undergoes in the course of the book is away from this tendency, towards a commitment to act practically in response to the particular needs of other people. The narrator affirms the necessity for such practical action, for 'even while we are talking and meditating about the earth's orbit and the solar system, what we feel and adjust our movements to is the stable earth and the changing day' (p. 525).

FREE INDIRECT STYLE

In Chapter 48, Casaubon, aware that his health is precarious, asks Dorothea to continue his work in the event of his death. She declines to commit herself, and requests that he allow her until the following day to make a decision. While he sleeps she lies awake, filled with dread at the prospect of a solitary life, engaged in labour which she now knows to be futile.

Twentieth century novelists, such as Virginia Woolf (1882–1941) and James Joyce (1882–1941), pioneered techniques of **interior monologue**, which granted readers direct access to the thoughts of a character. The conventions of the nineteenth century **realist** novel did not permit such bold entry into the workings of an individual consciousness, but George Eliot manages to render the conflict in Dorothea's mind through the voice of her omniscient narrator.

That voice reports Dorothea's inner turmoil, while also indicating the limits of her understanding. It remarks that 'she had no presentiment that the power which her husband wished to establish over her future action had relation to anything else than his work' (p. 478). This unilluminating comment assumes considerable significance following her husband's death, when it is revealed that a codicil added to his will prohibits her marriage to Will Ladislaw as long as she remains owner of Lowick Manor.

Dorothea has been disappointed in her hope of finding 'the fellowship in high knowledge which was to make life worthier'. Yet her sympathetic nature can still extend pity to the man who seeks to control her life even after his death. The narrative voice records questions she asks of herself: 'And had she not wished to marry him that she might help him in his life's labour?', and 'Was it right, even to soothe his grief – would it be possible, even if she promised – to work as in a treadmill fruitlessly?' (p. 479).

These questions are examples of a technique called **free indirect style**. The third person voice is still present, but it implies the first person. These are questions which Dorothea asks herself, but they are not presented directly. In interior monologue, the question 'And had she not wished to marry him that she might help him in his life's labour?' would appear as, 'Did I not wish to marry him in order to help him with his life's labour?'. Free indirect style allows George Eliot to filter the question through the voice of her **narrator**.

CHECK THE BOOK

Ann Banfield conducts a sophisticated examination of this technique in *Unspeakable Sentences: Narration and Representation of the Language of Fiction* (Routledge, 1982).

PART FOUR

CRITICAL PERSPECTIVES

READING CRITICALLY

This section provides a range of critical viewpoints and perspectives on *Middlemarch* and gives a broad overview of key debates, interpretations, and theories proposed since the novel was published. It is important to bear in mind the variety of interpretations and responses this text has produced, many of them shaped by the critics' own backgrounds and historical contexts.

No single view of the text should be seen as dominant – it is important that you arrive at your own judgements by questioning the perspectives described, and by developing your own critical insights. Objective analysis is a skill achieved through coupling close reading with an informed understanding of the key ideas, related texts, and background information relevant to the text. These elements are all crucial in enabling you to assess the interpretations of other readers, and even to view works of criticism as texts in themselves. The ability to read critically will serve you well both in your study of *Middlemarch*, and in any critical writing, presentation, or further work you undertake.

RECEPTION AND EARLY CRITICAL REVIEWS

Middlemarch first appeared in 1871–2. George Eliot had at that time established a reputation as England's leading novelist. The novel was eagerly anticipated, and expectation was heightened by the initial publication in parts at intervals. Literary magazines reviewed the parts as they appeared, caught up in the tensions of the unfolding plot.

Upon completion, George Eliot's friend Edith Simcox wrote an insightful review in the *Academy* in January 1873, noting the author's sustained focus on the 'inner life' of her characters, with events in the external world serving to support extended investigation of 'mental experience'. She also remarked upon parallels between Lydgate and Dorothea.

 **CHECK THE BOOK**

Critical evaluations of George Eliot, and of *Middlemarch*, have been conveniently collected in *A Century of George Eliot Criticism*, edited by G. S. Haight (Methuen, 1966); *George Eliot: The Critical Heritage*, edited by David Carroll (Routledge, 1971); and *Middlemarch: George Eliot*, edited by John Peck (Macmillan, 1992).

Henry James, who later became a major novelist, described *Middlemarch* as 'a treasure house of details', but 'an indifferent whole'. He found Ladislaw insubstantial, yet admired the portrayal of Lydgate, and approved of George Eliot's judicious handling of Casaubon's 'hollow pretentiousness and mouldy egotism'.

There was immediate critical uneasiness at the novel's pessimism, especially the absence of Christian consolation. R. H. Hutton, in the *Spectator*, admired the broad and accurate portrayal of provincial life, but commented on the novel's 'melancholy scepticism' and noted 'a certain air of moral desolation'. This perception of a basis for despair in her work contributed to a decline in George Eliot's popular and critical reputation from the end of the nineteenth century until the middle of the twentieth. In *The Cornhill Magazine*, in 1881, Leslie Stephen (father of the novelist Virginia Woolf) described *Middlemarch* as 'a rather painful book', and other readers around the turn of the century, including playwright George Bernard Shaw, found it excessively analytical and insufficiently optimistic.

CRITICAL HISTORY

George Eliot's reputation declined during the 1890s, and her earlier, less ambitious novels were far more widely read and discussed than *Middlemarch* and other later works, until the middle of the twentieth century. In 1919, 100 years after George Eliot's birth, Virginia Woolf wrote an essay about her for *The Times Literary Supplement*, which identified *Middlemarch* as the pinnacle of her achievement. But this view was not generally promoted until the influential Cambridge academic F. R. Leavis made the case for the novel's centrality to English literary history in *The Great Tradition* (1948).

Joan Bennett's *George Eliot: Her Mind and Her Art* was also published in 1948. Bennett stressed the importance of location. *Middlemarch* was Eliot's masterpiece because it brought her accumulated command of novelistic skills to bear on a region of England she knew intimately. The appearance of G. S. Haight's edition of George Eliot's letters during the 1950s gave added impetus to the renewed critical interest.

 CHECK THE BOOK
Karen Chase has edited a stimulating collection of new critical perspectives entitled *Middlemarch in the Twenty-First Century* (Oxford University Press, 2005). In her introduction she argues that although the text itself remains unchanged, 'its meaning changes both within the culture and within the consciousness of individual readers. It is for each generation to chart the differences that ensure that the novel will not become a relic' (p. 3).

CRITICAL HISTORY continued

 QUESTION

Jerome Beaty noted a tendency amongst readers to hope that Dorothea would end up married to Lydgate. Do you think their marriage would have been successful?

Barbara Hardy's *The Novels of George Eliot: A Study in Form* (1959) is an important work in the history of George Eliot criticism. Hardy traced the intricate patterning by means of which the novelist gave form to the copious materials of her fiction. The study refuted Henry James's claim that *Middlemarch* lacked overall control. W. J. Harvey's *The Art of George Eliot* (1961) also placed emphasis upon formal organisation.

Jerome Beaty's *Middlemarch: From Notebook to Novel*, published in 1960, was a scholarly investigation into the compositional process, unravelling the order of writing and of revising this large book. He draws on the author's preparatory planning for the novel, which had been published in 1950 as the *Quarry for 'Middlemarch'*, edited by A. T. Kitchel.

In *A Critical History of English Literature* (1960), David Daiches argued that George Eliot introduced a new seriousness into the English novel. Prior to her work the genre had been primarily entertainment, but she promoted moral and intellectual sophistication. *Middlemarch*, he found 'one of the very greatest of English novels', especially notable for its 'complex network of interrelationships'.

Publication of G. S. Haight's *George Eliot: A Biography*, in 1968, stimulated criticism based in biography. Another documentary resource, a collection of George Eliot's essays, edited by Thomas Pinney, had appeared in 1963.

Since the 1970s, George Eliot's work has been subjected to a range of contemporary critical approaches, including structuralism, Bahktinian analysis, and deconstruction. Feminist critics in particular have found her fiction a fertile arena for debate.

In 1979, the year before the centenary of her death, Hugh Witemeyer considered the novels in relation to other art forms in *George Eliot and the Visual Arts* (Yale University Press). Beryl Gray examined the novelist's engagement with music in *George Eliot and Music* (Macmillan, 1989). Sally Shuttleworth looked at the fiction in another cultural context in *George Eliot and Nineteenth-Century Science* (Cambridge University Press, 1984).

CONTEMPORARY APPROACHES

NEW HISTORICISM

New Historicism is not a narrow method but a broad approach to reading texts. The New Historicist critic aligns the literary work with other documents from the period, and by considering them together discloses social forces in operation. The writer may have been unaware of these forces, but they may nonetheless have shaped the composition of the text.

Middlemarch is clearly caught up in an ongoing debate on education. Rosamond Vincy is educated to be a decorative young lady, and although Dorothea Brooke's education is more substantial it still imposes severe limitations on her understanding of the ways of the world. Fred Vincy and Christy Garth both receive a university education, conventionally a necessity for the social advancement of young men. From 1869, Girton College, situated in Hitchin, mid way between London and Cambridge, offered more advanced education for young women. George Eliot made a financial contribution to its founding, although she was not unequivocal in her support for its aims.

A biographical critic might use her letters on the subject to cast light on the novel's handling of educational issues. A New Historicist critic would not feel bound to look for such personal materials, but might draw, for example, upon the documentation surrounding Forster's Education Act, which was passed by Parliament in 1870, the year before publication of *Middlemarch* began. The Act, which extended elementary education to all, meant an increase in the general level of literacy. It was surrounded by a mass of well documented argument. The novel might be read in relation to that discourse, and the critic might consider the implications of the fact that George Eliot was writing, at that time, a challenging, philosophically serious novel, which would pose a daunting prospect for a reading public that was about to grow rapidly.

 CHECK THE BOOK
Critical reading of a novel might be expected to focus primarily upon character. Kate Flint's essay 'The Materiality of *Middlemarch*', included in Karen Chase (ed.), *Middlemarch in the Twenty-First Century* (Oxford University Press, 2005), puts the emphasis instead upon the physical world within which the characters act. Flint's approach is that George Eliot was alert 'to the world of inanimate things, and to the emotions and values that get projected onto them' (p. 74).

Medical knowledge is also an evident concern of *Middlemarch*. Lydgate promotes a new understanding of the human body and is met with a largely hostile reaction. A New Historicist might collate documents elucidating advances in nineteenth century medicine, and then consider how new models offered by anatomy and physiology may be considered in relation to George Eliot's representation of human beings in her novel.

CONTEXT

Charles Darwin wrote in *On the Origin of Species* (1859), Chapter 3, that, 'Plants and animals, most remote in the scale of nature, are bound together by a complex web of relations.'

The **metaphor** of the web, which Lydgate admires in the work of the physiologist Bichat, assumes considerable structural and thematic importance in *Middlemarch* (see **Language and style: Metaphors**). It was a familiar metaphor in nineteenth century scientific thought, including the work of Charles Darwin. Important studies which may be said to assume a New Historicist orientation are Sally Shuttleworth's *George Eliot and Nineteenth-Century Science* (Cambridge University Press, 1984), which links George Eliot's theory of organic social evolution to ideas in nineteenth century physiology, and Gillian Beer's *Darwin's Plots* (Routledge, 1983), which relates the forms of Victorian fiction to emergent evolutionary theory.

A New Historicist reading might also fruitfully locate *Middlemarch* in relation to Victorian discourses of banking, philanthropy, or gambling, or in terms of the educational debates of the period.

FEMINIST CRITICISM

The term 'feminist criticism' covers a range of approaches crucially concerned with the representation of women, their personal identities, and their social relationships within a society dominated by men. A woman writer who assumed a man's name when publishing her work might be expected to exercise a particular fascination for feminist critics, but they have been divided in their response to George Eliot's work.

 CHECK THE BOOK

The 'formidable' presence George Eliot has achieved within the tradition of women's writing has been provocatively assessed by Elaine Showalter, in *A Literature of Their Own* (Virago, 1978).

George Eliot was unconventional, even radical, in the way she lived her own life, but her creation Dorothea Brooke becomes the self-sacrificing Mrs Casaubon, and after that chastening experience she surrenders herself to the requirements of being Mrs Ladislaw, wife and mother. Some critics have found that *Middlemarch* reproduces the dominant assumptions of patriarchal society, with no significant reversal of gender roles, and with the conventionally feminine virtue of passive compliance endorsed as a positive quality.

Middlemarch begins, admittedly, with reference to the willing martyrdom of Saint Theresa, but there are arguably important **ironies** being overlooked in this reading, and it is possible to discern a more actively feminist voice in the novel. For example, our attention is repeatedly drawn to the artificiality of Rosamond Vincy's training as a feminine woman, and although she appears obstinately childish and selfish, it is not difficult to make a case that she is a victim of patriarchal gender construction.

Rosamond has been manufactured as a social ornament, and has become an apparently insubstantial snob. But if her appearance did not conform to the prevalent definition of beauty, and if her parents were not so concerned for their children to become more elevated socially, she might have directed her intelligence and energies to more constructive ends. In their important feminist study *The Madwoman in the Attic* (Yale University Press, 1979), Sandra Gilbert and Susan Gubar identify Rosamond Vincy as George Eliot's most important rebellious female, and argue that when she and Dorothea have their emotional encounter near the end of *Middlemarch*, they seem childish because their full maturity has been denied by imposed femininity.

Gillian Beer, in *George Eliot* (Harvester Press, 1980) also makes the case that Rosamond was entrapped by patriarchal views. She surveys earlier feminist work on George Eliot, and affirms that although she was not a militant participant in the woman's movement she was aware of the key issues of contemporary debate, and fed them into *Middlemarch*. Jennifer Uglow, in *George Eliot* (Virago, 1987) finds her a more tentative feminist, who endorsed the perpetuation of certain established female values, and was ambivalent towards organised feminism.

Post-structuralist criticism

A few decades ago, an array of theoretical positions became apparent, primarily in French academic circles, which has become

CHECK THE BOOK
A stimulating critical analysis is offered by Laura Morgan Green in *Educating Women: Cultural Conflict and Victorian Literature* (Ohio University Press, 2001). She points out that George Eliot had reservations about Emily Davies's plan to emulate the set-up of a male college at Cambridge in her new establishment for women. Green argues that Casaubon is presented **satirically** as the musty outcome of a traditional education at an Oxford or Cambridge college.

known as post-structuralism. These diverse theories have in common a disregard for the intentions of the author, and an emphasis upon the play of language within a text. The post-structuralist critic is not interested in what George Eliot wanted her novel to signify. Rather, the focus is upon the text as a structure of signs, whose meaning is inherently unstable.

In other words, not only is *Middlemarch* not governed by George Eliot's intention, but structures of meaning within the language of the text are themselves inconsistent or contradictory. We may not in the usual course of reading be aware of these inconsistencies and contradictions. The post-structuralist critic understands them to be an inevitable byproduct of the nature of language.

CHECK THE BOOK

A distinguished demonstration of this form of criticism is *Blindness and Insight* by Paul De Man (Oxford University Press, 1971).

One of the prominent manifestations of post-structuralism is deconstruction, a critical practice that takes its lead from the work of the French philosopher Jacques Derrida (1930–2004). Deconstruction is a practice of exposing how texts break the very laws of structuring and expression that permit them to exist, undermining their apparent meaning, and calling their authoritative status into question.

In a broad application of Paul De Man's approach, we might return to the passage used for **Extended commentaries: Text 1**. That passage presents an image of a pier-glass, or mirror, which is covered with haphazard scratches. The **narrator** remarks that if you place a lighted candle against it, the scratches appear to form themselves into a series of concentric circles. It is the candle that produces the illusion of concentric arrangement, through a process of optical selection. As George Eliot puts it, 'The scratches are events, and the candle is the egoism of any person now absent' (p. 264). This is a **metaphor** that suggests that events assume the semblance of order through the action of the perceiver or interpreter, rather than being intrinsically ordered.

This insight discloses the importance of point of view in *Middlemarch*. Instead of reality being a self-evident order of truth, it now appears to be the product of multiple interpretations, overlapping but never identical. Individual egos preside over concentric circles of meaning, but these are not contained within an overall unitary order, and consequently characters clash in their view of things and are often troubled by mutual misunderstanding. Following De Man's example, we might point out George Eliot's inconsistency in deploying an **omniscient narrator** to furnish this insight.

Preserving the all-knowing voice, she sought to hold together a fictional world that is inherently fragmented. We might say that she sought to affirm the presence of God, despite her avowed agnosticism. It might also be shown that the identity of this omniscient narrator is less unified than it initially appears. Not only are there apparent inconsistencies in its observations, but the voice itself assumes at times a markedly different character, which might be taken to register internal divisions. We could argue that the semblance of omniscience is preserved, only to be discredited by the metaphor of the candle and the mirror. Thus, deconstruction subverts the narrative's claim to unity and coherence beyond the play of language.

CHECK THE BOOK

A sophisticated deconstructive reading can be found in J. Hillis Miller's 'Optic and semiotic in Middlemarch', in *The Worlds of Victorian Fiction*, edited by Jerome Buckley (Harvard University Press, 1975).

PART FIVE

BACKGROUND

GEORGE ELIOT'S LIFE AND WORKS

'George Eliot' was the assumed name of Mary Ann Evans, who was born on 22 November 1819, at South Farm, Arbury, in Warwickshire. Her father, Robert Evans, managed the estate of Francis Newdigate. Her mother, Christiana Pearson, was Evans's second wife. Mary Ann had an older sister and brother, Christiana and Isaac.

Soon after her birth, the family moved to Griff House, on another part of the estate. Mary Ann started school in 1824. Her formal education continued until 1836, when her mother's illness and subsequent death brought it to an end. The following year she became her father's housekeeper, but through her own efforts, and by arranging lessons with tutors from Coventry, she continued to study Greek, Latin, Italian, French, and German.

As a child, Mary Ann was ardently religious. In 1840 her faith remained strong and she published a poem in the *Christian Observer*. Then, in 1841, she and her father moved to Coventry, enabling Isaac to take over Griff House, following his marriage. She entered a circle of sceptics and freethinkers, and early in 1842 her refusal to attend church resulted in temporary estrangement from her father. She remained a sceptic and agnostic throughout the rest of her life, yet was interested in controversial works of contemporary theology. In January 1844, she began a translation from German of David Strauss's *The Life of Jesus*, eventually published anonymously in 1846.

In 1849 her father died, leaving her a small guaranteed income for the rest of her life. She travelled in Europe, with her liberal friends Charles and Cara Bray. At this time, she changed her name to 'Marianne', then 'Marian'. In 1850, she contributed her first article to the *Westminster Review*. In September 1851, she became its assistant editor, mingling with the leading thinkers of the day. She

 CHECK THE BOOK
A very useful consideration of George Eliot in the social and intellectual context of her time is Tim Dolin's *George Eliot: Authors in Context* (Oxford University Press, 2005).

CONTEXT
In 1845 George Eliot received a proposal of marriage from a picture-restorer, whose name is not known.

developed a close friendship with the philosopher, Herbert Spencer (1820–1903). In October 1851, she first encountered George Henry Lewes (1817–78), writer, philosopher, and scientist. They fell in love, but Lewes was already married, and although separated from his wife, he was unable to secure a divorce. Nonetheless, Lewes and Evans lived together as husband and wife. It was a bold decision, considered immoral by most people at that time. Her brother had no further contact with her until after Lewes's death.

In 1854, Mary Ann Evans's translation of Ludwig Feuerbach's controversial study *The Essence of Christianity* was published. In July she travelled to Germany, where Lewes worked on his *Life of Goethe* and she wrote articles. On their return to London in 1855, they continued to live together, gradually winning acceptance for that arrangement. By 1877, their social prestige was such that they dined with Princess Louise. Lewes died in November 1878.

In 1857, the stories collected as *Scenes of Clerical Life* began to appear in *Blackwood's Magazine*. It was at this time that she took the pseudonym, 'George Eliot'. The name change may have been partly defensive, concealing the authorship of Mary Ann Evans (now calling herself Marian), who was living scandalously with George Lewes. But there seems to have been a conscious decision to lay claim to the authority reserved for men in a patriarchal society, and to circumvent the assumptions that awaited fiction written by a woman. She did, of course, write as a woman, but increasingly with a seriousness conventionally considered masculine.

Her fiction grew increasingly challenging and complex, culminating in *Middlemarch*, her epic of provincial life, and her sophisticated novel of Jewish culture, *Daniel Deronda* (1876). The earlier novels *Adam Bede* (1859), *The Mill on the Floss* (1860), and *Silas Marner* (1861) are more immediately accessible, but they establish some of her enduring concerns. In *Adam Bede*, her commitment to literary **realism** was already clear, in a portrait of rural English life that explores the nature of human sympathy. *The Mill on the Floss* anticipates *Middlemarch* in its account of the effect of the narrowness of provincial life upon young people with aspirations. *Silas Marner* is also a tale of dreams and disillusionment.

 CHECK THE BOOK

Charlotte Brontë's second novel, *Shirley* (1849) is set against the outbreak of violence in the Yorkshire textile industry.

CHECK THE BOOK

A magisterial account of working class lives during the years 1780 and 1832 is E. P. Thompson's *The Making of the English Working Class* (Penguin Books, 1991; 1963).

Her travels in Europe broadened George Eliot's horizons and furnished material for her historical novel, *Romola* (1863), which is set in Italy. In *Middlemarch* she combined Roman episodes with her study of the English Midlands at the time of the first Reform Act. *Felix Holt, the Radical* (1866) is focused on those political issues, leading to the passing of the Act in 1832, as they reverberate through ordinary lives. George Eliot's fiction sustains a remarkable level of achievement, but *Middlemarch* is widely held to be her creative peak.

On 6 May 1880, Evans surprised her friends by marrying J. W. ('Johnny') Cross, an American banker, more than twenty years her junior. Shortly after moving with him to central London, she fell ill, and on 22 December she died from pneumonia, aged sixty-one years. She is buried in Highgate Cemetery, North London, alongside G. H. Lewes.

In 1885, J. W. Cross published *George Eliot's Life: As Related in Her Letters and Journals*. Cross edited the materials carefully to ensure that his late wife appeared conventionally virtuous. The result is a very partial portrait, and some who knew her remarked that it made her seem dull, which in life she never was.

Eliot's *Letters*, edited by G. S. Haight, were published in nine volumes by Oxford University Press, between 1954 and 1978. Haight's *George Eliot: A Biography* (Oxford University Press, 1968) has long been regarded as the standard biographical work. An important recent biography is Frederick Karl's *George Eliot* (HarperCollins, 1995).

HISTORICAL BACKGROUND

Middlemarch was written between 1869 and 1871, but the story is set in the years 1829 to 1832. The intervening period had wrought significant changes in the nature of English society, and had witnessed more fundamental changes in the way the world was understood by scientists and philosophers. An important critical distance is established by those forty years separating the fictional action from the actual writing of the novel. It enabled George Eliot to indicate to her initial readers ongoing processes of social change.

ECONOMIC AND DEMOGRAPHIC CHANGE

By 1815, Parliament had sanctioned the enclosure of common land, extending the property rights of wealthy landowners while dispossessing those who had previously farmed the open fields. Some became tenant farmers dependent for their well-being upon the conscience of a landowner. In *Middlemarch*, we can see that those at Freshitt benefit from Chettam's enlightened view, while others, like Dagley who lives and works on Brooke's land, are less fortunate.

The industrial revolution during the late eighteenth and early nineteenth centuries caused dramatic changes to the way work was organised, not just in factories but in agriculture too. The threshing machine, which separated grain from stalks, revolutionised harvesting. Such innovations made many rural workers less valuable to potential employers. Seasonal jobs became more scarce and were often less well remunerated. There was a trend for country people to move into the growing towns and cities in search of employment in manufacturing industries, such as the one Mr Vincy owns. Working conditions were often appalling. The aristocratic Mrs Cadwallader vitriolically refers to Vincy as 'one of those who suck the life out of the wretched handloom weavers in Tipton and Freshitt' (p. 327).

The arrival of the railway accelerated this movement from country to town, transforming the overall basis of the English economy from agriculture to industry. It also led to serious overcrowding, which in poorly sanitised areas resulted often in the spread of disease. The process of rural depopulation led to a drift of social power and influence, away from the upper classes towards members of the middle classes such as Nicholas Bulstrode.

Workers who remained in rural areas became increasingly desperate. Some lapsed into theft; the case of a man sentenced to be hanged for stealing a sheep is mentioned in Chapter 4 of *Middlemarch*.

In 1830 the so-called Swing Riots occurred in the south and east of England, in protest against the adverse impact of the threshing

 CHECK THE POEM
The poet John Clare (1793–1864) lamented the passing of the Enclosure Act in his poem 'The Mores': 'Enclosure came and trampled on the grave / Of labour's rights and left the poor a slave' (lines 19–20).

HISTORICAL BACKGROUND

ECONOMIC AND DEMOGRAPHIC CHANGE continued

CHECK THE BOOK

Eric Hobsbawm and George Rudé tell the story of these riots in *Captain Swing: A Social History of the Great English Agricultural Uprising of 1830* (Pimlico Books, 1993; 1973).

machine. Barns where tithes were stored were destroyed, hayricks set ablaze, machines smashed. The government reacted harshly – nine rioters were hanged, 450 sent as convicts to Australia.

In the towns and cities of the industrial Midlands and north of England there had been comparable disturbances. Over the course of a few years, starting in 1811, discontented workers, commonly known as the Luddites, destroyed mechanised looms and other machinery that threatened their livelihood.

The movement for Reform which is presented in Middlemarch was not simply altruistic; there was widespread recognition that discontent amongst the working poor had to be contained and defused in order to prevent the possibility of serious social upheaval of the kind France had witnessed. Measures such as the Poor Law Amendment Act of 1834 were beneficial to the poor, but they also removed some potentially destabilising sources of discontent.

POLITICAL AND RELIGIOUS REFORM

The demographic shift from the countryside to the city highlighted inconsistencies and absurdities in the system of parliamentary representation. Rapidly expanding industrial towns, and even cities like Birmingham and Manchester, were unrepresented in Parliament, while rural regions retained their traditional enfranchisement. There persisted in these regions 'rotten boroughs', which returned a member to Parliament despite being almost uninhabited, and 'pocket boroughs' where voting was controlled by a single landowner. Electoral corruption and inequality is discussed in the opening pages of Chapter 37.

The First Reform Act, promoted by the Prime Minister Lord Grey and his Home Secretary Lord John Russell, became law in June 1832. It reformed the electoral system, enabling the middle classes to participate much more extensively in government. Still, the working class and a substantial proportion of the lower middle class remained unenfranchised. It was not until 1867 that Benjamin Disraeli's Second Reform Act extended voting rights to working class men in towns and cities. Agricultural workers had to await the

Third Reform Act, in 1884–5. Women of all classes were excluded from the franchise until the twentieth century.

There are numerous references in *Middlemarch* to 'the Catholic question'. Roman Catholics were excluded from public office, from university education, and from commissions in the armed forces.

The Anglican monopoly of positions of power, institutionalised through the Test and Corporations Acts, also excluded dissenting Protestants. In 1829, the Whig politician Lord John Russell pushed a bill through Parliament repealing the Acts. Advantages were extended to dissenters, but not to Roman Catholics, a relatively small group in England. In Ireland the majority of the population were Catholic, and they protested energetically at being excluded from any form of political representation. Sir Robert Peel, Home Secretary in the Tory government led by the Duke of Wellington, passed the Roman Catholic Relief Act in 1829, granting Catholics the same rights as the Protestant dissenters.

Throughout her adult life, George Eliot was an agnostic, unable to sustain belief in orthodox religious doctrines. In this respect, her experience was typical of many middle class intellectuals of the Victorian period. Her early faith was eroded by her exposure to the arguments of scientific rationalism and to critical readings of the Bible offered by contemporary progressive scholarship. The years 1829–32, in which *Middlemarch* is set, correspond closely to the critical time in her own response to Christian orthodoxy.

SCIENCE AND THE MEDICAL PROFESSION

Medical education underwent substantial change during the course of the nineteenth century. A new training school at University College London opened in 1828. Other London hospitals established medical schools during the 1830s. Most medical education at that point was provided by established practitioners – not necessarily the best teachers as their mistakes were then replicated by their students.

George Eliot reflects contemporary debates surrounding treatment and diagnosis. Lydgate's qualifications, his theories, and his practice

---

CONTEXT

Robert Peel (1788–1850), Home Secretary (p. 9), initially opposed extension to Roman Catholics of the right to become Members of Parliament and then supported it. This issue is discussed in Chapters 1 and 71.

CONTEXT

It was a huge step forward for the medical profession to recognise that infectious illness is caused by organisms not visible to the naked eye. Key figures in germ theory were the French microbiologist Louis Pasteur (1822–95) and the German physician Robert Koch (1843–1910). Pasteur's work led English physician Joseph Lister (1827–1912) to introduce antiseptic practices into surgery during the 1860s.

SCIENCE AND THE MEDICAL PROFESSION continued

are all points of contention. He runs into conflict with Sprague and Minchin, the established practitioners for the region. They have been authorised by the Royal College of Physicians, an institution for which Lydgate has little time. They are disturbed that he does not conform to the pattern of the surgeon-apothecary that had been continued by Mr Peacock his predecessor, and is reflected in the approach of Mr Wrench.

Lydgate's modern outlook is shown in his use of a stethoscope, which was by no means common practice at that time. He is inspired by Vesalius, founder of modern anatomy, and by the French physiologist, Bichat, and he views the new hospital not merely as a place to tend the sick, but as a centre for research. Popular misapprehension is exemplified by Mrs Dollop, landlady of the Tankard inn, who speculates that Lydgate may allow patients to die in order to anatomise their dead bodies (p. 442).

More generally science was transforming the known world, through its impact upon technological innovation and through new conceptual models of the nature of physical reality. Charles Lyell (1797–1875) published his *Principles of Geology* in three volumes between 1830 and 1833, arguing that geological processes presently occurring in the world enable us to understand how such processes have in the past shaped the Earth. This work exerted considerable influence upon the zoologist Charles Darwin (1809–82), whose theory of evolution, outlined in *On the Origin of Species* (1859) and *The Descent of Man* (1871) posed a radical challenge to both scientific and religious orthodoxies.

Around the time George Eliot was working on *Middlemarch*, eminent Scottish scientist James Clark Maxwell (1831–79) crossed the threshold into modern physics, formulating his kinetic theory of gases by means of a statistical method that carried scientific analysis far beyond what is physically observable. A comparably bold advance beyond the human sensory realm had been made in microbiology when French scientist Louis Pasteur (1822–95) developed the germ theory of disease. Just as agricultural labourers were uprooted from the land during the nineteenth century, intellectuals were progressively uprooted from traditional ways of

CONTEXT

The Anatomy Act of 1832 made it easier for medical researchers to acquire corpses for dissection. Prior to that only executed murderers could legally be used for such a purpose. During the early nineteenth century there were fewer executions than before and at the same time there was increased demand for cadavers for medical research. In a notorious case in 1828 and 1829 William Burke and William Hare committed a series of seventeen murders and sold the bodies of their victims to Edinburgh Medical College for dissection.

understanding the world. Such was the unsettled cultural climate in which George Eliot wrote.

LITERARY BACKGROUND

HENRY FIELDING

In Chapter 15, the **narrator** alludes to 'a great historian', who has taken 'his place amongst the colossi whose huge legs our living pettiness is observed to walk under' (p. 141). The reference is to Henry Fielding (1707–54), a writer who set the course the English novel would take for a hundred years. His great work, *Tom Jones* (1749), is comparable to *Middlemarch* in its scope and technical achievement, although the England it depicts is markedly different. One reason for the **allusion** is to draw our attention to historical change. George Eliot's novel portrays the arrival of a more hurried and money-driven society.

Her narrator refers especially to Fielding's tendency to indulge in 'copious remarks and digressions' (p. 141), making direct address to his readers. He made no attempt to conceal his own voice as it delivered moral guidance, drawing large conclusions applicable to the world as a whole. *Middlemarch* follows his example in its use of an **omniscient narrator**, passing comment on the action of the novel, but it would be wrong to identify this narrator as a firmly didactic authorial voice of the kind Fielding employed.

The **narrative voice** in *Middlemarch* is less assured and less consistent. It is omniscient in the sense that it assumes access to characters' thoughts, and can report separate events occurring simultaneously, but its interpretations always imply that another point of view is possible. The narrator concludes:

> I at least have so much to do in unravelling certain human lots, and seeing how they were woven and interwoven, that all the light I can command must be concentrated on this particular web, and not dispersed over that tempting range of relevancies called the universe. (p. 141)

> **CONTEXT**
>
> The General Medical Council came into being in 1858 to control qualifications and, increasingly, to regularise practice.

CHECK THE BOOK

A Doll's House (1879) by Norwegian dramatist Henrik Ibsen (1828–1906) is a controversial play that presents, like *Middlemarch*, a woman dissatisfied with the confining role assigned to a middle class wife. Ibsen's main character Nora Helmer, a mother of three, married to a banker, rejects the stifling atmosphere and leaves her family. Although George Eliot's own life was highly unconventional she makes Dorothea Brooke a far less radical figure than Nora Helmer or Flaubert's Emma Bovary.

The capacity to pass judgement with absolute confidence has been lost.

THE NINETEENTH-CENTURY NOVEL

From the point of view of the literary historian, the novel in the early years of the nineteenth century was dominated by the social satires of Jane Austen (1775–1817) and the historical novels of Sir Walter Scott (1771–1832). In Victorian England, William Makepeace Thackeray (1811–63), Charles Dickens (1812–70), and Anthony Trollope (1815–82) achieved great popular success with their novels portraying modern manners or addressing pressing issues of the day in an entertaining fashion. Their achievement was considerable, but elsewhere the novel was being conceived as a more self-consciously serious form of literary art.

Gustave Flaubert (1821–80) raised the French novel to a new level of refinement and **realism**. The sophisticated Russian writer Ivan Turgenev (1818–83), who paid regular visits to George Eliot's home, achieved a comparable degree of seriousness. Such elevated aspirations entered the English tradition with the later work of George Eliot, signalling the way for developments in fiction in the early decades of the twentieth century. Her work aims for accurate representation of social reality, encompassing class and gender relationships, varieties of religious belief, technological and intellectual developments, as well as depiction of the physical conditions of everyday life.

In *Middlemarch* George Eliot portrays the life of a community just as her older contemporary Elizabeth Gaskell (1810–65) had in her novel *Cranford* (1851) but the scope is far broader. *Cranford* is an astute and charming novel of village life. *Middlemarch* is the **epic** depiction of a region and a phase of history, and an attempt to register valuable truths about the conduct of human life at a historical juncture when truth had become a problematic concept. The intellectual scale and historical dimension of *Middlemarch* bears comparison with the epic social realism of the great Russian novelist Lev Tolstoy (1828–1910) in *War and Peace* (1869) and *Anna Karenina* (1877).

World events

1866 War between Austria and Prussia; Russell ministry resigns after defeat of Reform Bill; Derby forms Conservative ministry with Disraeli as leader of the House of Commons

1867 Second Reform Bill passed by Parliament, adding nearly one million to the electorate; Fenian rising in Ireland; USA buys Alaska from Russia; Lister's use of carbolic antiseptic reduces risk of infection in surgery; Nobel patents dynamite

1868 Gladstone becomes Liberal Prime Minister; first annual Trade Union Congress in Manchester

1869 Anglican Church disestablished in Ireland; Suez Canal opened; first transcontinental American railway completed; *Cutty Sark* launched

1870 Outbreak of the Franco-Prussian War (–1871); siege of Paris; Gladstone's first Irish Land Act passed; first Married Women's Property Act gives wives right to keep their earnings; diamond mining starts in South Africa; death of Charles Dickens

Author's life

1866 *Felix Holt, The Radical* published

1867 Travels around Spain with G. H. Lewes

1868 Returns from Spain and begins to live with G. H. Lewes as his wife; *The Spanish Gypsy* published

1869 *Agatha: A Poem* published; work on a story about a provincial town called Middlemarch begins; second son of G. H. Lewes, Thornie, dies

1870 The first ten chapters of *Middlemarch*, as we know it, are written

Literary events

1866 Carlyle, *On the Choice of Books*; Dostoevsky, *Crime and Punishment*; Gaskell, *Wives and Daughters*; Rossetti, C., *The Prince's Progress and other Poems*

1867 Arnold, *On the Study of Celtic Literature*; *New Poems*; Marx, *Das Kapital*; Ruskin, *Time and Tide*; Tolstoy, *War and Peace* (completed 1869)

1868 Alcott, *Little Women*; Queen Victoria, *Leaves from a Journal of Our Life in the Highlands*; Browning, *The Ring and the Book*

1869 Arnold, *Culture and Anarchy*; *Collected Poems*; Blackmore, *Lorna Doone*; Flaubert, *Sentimental Education*; Mill, *On the Subjection of Women*; Tennyson, *The Holy Grail, and Other Poems*

1870 Dickens, *The Mystery of Edwin Drood, Speeches, Literary and Social*; Disraeli, *Lothair*; Huxley, T. H., *Sermons, Addresses and Reviews*; Ruskin, *Lectures on Art*; Verne, *Twenty Thousand Leagues under the Sea*; Swinburne, *Ode on the Proclamation of a French Republic*

World events

1871 Prussia victorious over France; Paris Commune suppressed; in Britain, Trade Union Act makes picketing illegal; bill passed abolishing religious tests at Oxford and Cambridge Universities allowing attendance by non-Anglicans; Darwin, *The Descent of Man*

1872 Ballot Act secures secret voting; National Labourer's Union founded; Monet, *Impression, Sunrise*

1873 Agricultural and financial depression starts throughout Britain; first commercially successful typewriter designed in America; invention of barbed wire in America

1874 Disraeli becomes Conservative PM (–1880); Building Societies Act encourages home ownership

1875 Social reforms of Disraeli's administration include Public Health Act, Artisans' Dwelling Act and Sale of Food and Drugs Act; Disraeli buys Britain shares in the Suez Canal; completion of London's main drainage system

Author's life

1871 The story set in Middlemarch begun in 1869 and the story of Miss Brooke written in 1870 are married together to form *Middlemarch*; in December the first part of *Middlemarch* is published

1872 *Middlemarch* is a commercial and critical success; in December a four volume edition of the work is published

1873 'Guinea Edition' of *Middlemarch* published in March

1874 *The Legend of Jubal and Other Poems* published; serialisation of *Daniel Deronda* begun

1875 *Daniel Deronda* continues to be serialised, and George Eliot is now firmly recognised as the greatest living English novelist

Literary events

1871 Lewis Carroll, *Through the Looking Glass*; Meredith, *The Adventures of Harry Richmond*; Ruskin, *Fors Calvigera*; *Letters to the Workmen and Labourers of Great Britain*; Lear, *Nonsense Songs and Stories*

1872 Hardy, *Under the Greenwood Tree*; Nietzsche, *The Birth of Tragedy*; Browning, R., *Fifine at the Fair*; Lear, *More Nonsense Songs*; Tennyson, *Gareth and Lynette*

1873 Arnold, *Literature and Dogma*; Hardy, *A Pair of Blue Eyes*; Spencer, *The Study of Sociology*; Browning, R., *Red Cotton Night-Cap Country*

1874 Hardy, *Far From the Madding Crowd*; Ruskin, *Val d'Arno*; Wordsworth, D., *Recollections of a Tour Made in Scotland*

1875 Arnold, *God and the Bible*; Trollope, *The Way We Live Now*; Browning R., *Aristophanes' Apology*; *The Inn Album*; Morris, *The Aeneid of Virgil* (trans.); Tennyson, *The Lover's Tale*

FURTHER READING

OTHER WORKS BY GEORGE ELIOT

Scenes of Clerical Life (1858)

Adam Bede (1859)

The Mill on the Floss (1860)

Silas Marner (1861)

Romola (1863)

Felix Holt (1866)

Daniel Deronda (1876)

George Eliot's fiction is available in paperback editions published by Penguin Books.

BIOGRAPHIES

Rosemary Ashton, *George Eliot: A Life*, Penguin Books, 1998

> An insightful critical biography by a leading George Eliot scholar

Gordon S. Haight, *George Eliot: A Biography*, Oxford University Press, 1968

> The authoritative account of George Eliot's life

Jenny Uglow, *George Eliot*, Virago, 2008; 1987

> Uglow pays particular attention to George Eliot's unorthodox lifestyle and to the relative conformity she allocates to her female characters

GENERAL READING

Gillian Beer, *Darwin's Plots: Evolutionary Narrative in Darwin, George Eliot and Nineteenth-Century Fiction*, Routledge, 1983

> Chapter Five presents a stimulating discussion of *Middlemarch* in relation to Darwin's evolutionary theory

Tim Dolin, *George Eliot: Authors in Context*, Oxford University Press, 2005

> A useful placing of George Eliot in the cultural contexts of her time

Eric Hobsbawm, *The Age of Revolution, 1789–1848*, Vintage, 1996

> A penetrating historical analysis of the impact of the French Revolution and the Industrial Revolution upon the societies of Western Europe

George Levine (ed.), *The Cambridge Companion to George Eliot*, Cambridge University Press, 2001

> Specially commissioned essays that form an authoritative overview of George Eliot's life and work

FURTHER READING

John Rignall (ed.), *Oxford Reader's Companion to George Eliot*, Oxford University Press, 2001
> A detailed overview of George Eliot, her life, her work, and its historical context

E. P. Thompson, *The Making of the English Working Class*, Penguin Books, 1991
> An authoritative and stimulating account of the artisan and working class in its formative years, 1780 to 1832

Raymond Williams, *The Country and the City*, Oxford University Press, 1975
> Insightful readings of a range of English literature against a social background of demographic shift from rural to urban environments

CRITICAL STUDIES

Lucie Armitt (ed.), *Icon Critical Guide to George Eliot : Adam Bede, The Mill on the Floss, Middlemarch*, Icon, 2000
> A variety of critical perspectives upon *Middlemarch* and two earlier George Eliot novels

Karen Chase, *George Eliot: 'Middlemarch'*, Cambridge University Press, 1991
> Pays particular attention to the role and status of women

Karen Chase (ed.), *Middlemarch in the Twenty-First Century*, Oxford University Press, 2005
> Collects sophisticated and adventurous interpretations by leading scholars, including Gillian Beer and J. Hillis Miller

Barbara Hardy, *Particularities: Readings in George Eliot*, Peter Owen, 1982
> Shrewd readings of George Eliot by one of her most insightful critics

John Peck (ed.), *Middlemarch: George Eliot*, Macmillan, 1992
> A well chosen selection of critical approaches to *Middlemarch*

Sally Shuttleworth, *George Eliot and Nineteenth-Century Science: The Make-Believe of a Beginning*, Cambridge University Press, 1984
> Ponders the notion of organic social evolution in relation to Eliot's work

allegory a story or a situation with two different meanings, where the straightforward meaning on the surface is used to **symbolise** a deeper meaning underneath. This secondary meaning is often a spiritual or moral one whose values are represented by specific figures, characters, or events in the **narrative**

allusion (alludes) passing reference in a work of literature to something outside the text; may include other works of literature, **myth**, historical facts, or biographical detail

analogy a correspondence in certain respects between things that are otherwise different

caricature a representation distorted sufficiently to make its object appear comical or absurd

dialect manner of speaking a language, particular to a locality

epic long **narrative** work which aspires to encompass all aspects of an epoch or a nation

epigraph a quotation placed at the start of a literary work to focus attention on the meaning of what follows

flashback term taken from cinema, signifying a sudden jump back to an earlier episode or scene

free indirect style a blend of third and first person **narrative**, which in effect filters the thoughts of a character through the voice of a **narrator**

historical novel a fiction set in the past, mingling real and imaginary characters

interior monologue a technique for rendering the flow of thoughts within a character's mind

idiom a word or phrase specific to the language or culture from which it comes, which has a different meaning from what is expected

irony the quality of an utterance or an event which appears to signify one thing but in fact conveys a meaning other than the obvious

legend story about a heroic figure

melodrama writing which relies upon sensational happenings, violent action, and improbable events

metaphor one thing described as being another thing, and consequently assuming some of its associations

myth story which explains the nature of things, without reference to historical circumstances

narrative a story, tale, or any recital of events, and the manner in which it is told. First person narratives ('I') are told from the character's perspective and usually require the reader to judge carefully what is being said; second person narratives ('you') suggest the reader is part of the story; in third person narratives ('he', 'she', 'they') the narrator may be intrusive (continually commenting on the story), impersonal, or **omniscient**. More than one style of narrative may be used in a text

narrative voice an explicit or implied person telling a story

LITERARY TERMS

narrator the voice telling the story or narrating a sequence of events

omniscient narrator a **narrator** who uses the third person **narrative** and has a god-like knowledge of events and of the thoughts and feelings of the characters

parable simple story which delivers a moral or lesson

paradox a seemingly absurd or self-contradictory statement that is or may be true

personify to attribute human qualities to something

pun two different meanings drawn from a single word

realism set of conventions which enables representation of knowable communities and knowable characters

rhetorical question a question asked for emphasis rather than enquiry

Romantic term applied to philosophical beliefs and artistic practices fashionable in Europe at the end of the eighteenth and beginning of the nineteenth centuries

satire a type of literature in which folly, evil, or topical issues are held up to scorn through ridicule, **irony**, or exaggeration

simile overt comparison of one thing with another, in order to disclose shared attributes

social satire literature which mockingly exposes the flaws and foibles of society

symbolism investing material objects with abstract powers and meanings greater than their own; allowing a complex idea to be represented by a single object

type a representative figure

AUTHOR OF THESE NOTES

Julian Cowley holds degrees from University College London (BA Hons), the Institute of United States Studies, University of London (MA), and King's College London (PhD). After lecturing for fifteen years he is now a freelance writer and the author of several York Notes Advanced titles including *The Great Gatsby* and *Persuasion*.

GCSE

Maya Angelou
I Know Why the Caged Bird Sings

Jane Austen
Pride and Prejudice

Alan Ayckbourn
Absent Friends

Elizabeth Barrett Browning
Selected Poems

Robert Bolt
A Man for All Seasons

Harold Brighouse
Hobson's Choice

Charlotte Brontë
Jane Eyre

Emily Brontë
Wuthering Heights

Brian Clark
Whose Life is it Anyway?

Robert Cormier
Heroes

Shelagh Delaney
A Taste of Honey

Charles Dickens
David Copperfield
Great Expectations
Hard Times
Oliver Twist
Selected Stories

Roddy Doyle
Paddy Clarke Ha Ha Ha

George Eliot
Silas Marner
The Mill on the Floss

Anne Frank
The Diary of a Young Girl

William Golding
Lord of the Flies

Oliver Goldsmith
She Stoops to Conquer

Willis Hall
The Long and the Short and the Tall

Thomas Hardy
Far from the Madding Crowd
The Mayor of Casterbridge
Tess of the d'Urbervilles
The Withered Arm and other Wessex Tales

L. P. Hartley
The Go-Between

Seamus Heaney
Selected Poems

Susan Hill
I'm the King of the Castle

Barry Hines
A Kestrel for a Knave

Louise Lawrence
Children of the Dust

Harper Lee
To Kill a Mockingbird

Laurie Lee
Cider with Rosie

Arthur Miller
The Crucible
A View from the Bridge

Robert O'Brien
Z for Zachariah

Frank O'Connor
My Oedipus Complex and Other Stories

George Orwell
Animal Farm

J. B. Priestley
An Inspector Calls
When We Are Married

Willy Russell
Educating Rita
Our Day Out

J. D. Salinger
The Catcher in the Rye

William Shakespeare
Henry IV Part I
Henry V
Julius Caesar
Macbeth
The Merchant of Venice
A Midsummer Night's Dream
Much Ado About Nothing
Romeo and Juliet
The Tempest
Twelfth Night

George Bernard Shaw
Pygmalion

Mary Shelley
Frankenstein

R. C. Sherriff
Journey's End

Rukshana Smith
Salt on the Snow

John Steinbeck
Of Mice and Men

Robert Louis Stevenson
Dr Jekyll and Mr Hyde

Jonathan Swift
Gulliver's Travels

Robert Swindells
Daz 4 Zoe

Mildred D. Taylor
Roll of Thunder, Hear My Cry

Mark Twain
Huckleberry Finn

James Watson
Talking in Whispers

Edith Wharton
Ethan Frome

William Wordsworth
Selected Poems
A Choice of Poets
Mystery Stories of the Nineteenth Century including The Signalman
Nineteenth Century Short Stories
Poetry of the First World War
Six Women Poets

For the AQA Anthology:
Duffy and Armitage & Pre-1914 Poetry
Heaney and Clarke & Pre-1914 Poetry
Poems from Different Cultures

Key Stage 3

William Shakespeare
Much Ado About Nothing
Richard III
The Tempest

Margaret Atwood
Cat's Eye
The Handmaid's Tale

Jane Austen
Emma
Mansfield Park
Persuasion
Pride and Prejudice
Sense and Sensibility

Pat Barker
Regeneration

William Blake
Songs of Innocence and of Experience

The Brontës
Selected Poems

Charlotte Brontë
Jane Eyre
Villette

Emily Brontë
Wuthering Heights

Angela Carter
The Bloody Chamber
Nights at the Circus
Wise Children

Geoffrey Chaucer
The Franklin's Prologue and Tale
The Merchant's Prologue and Tale
The Miller's Prologue and Tale
The Prologue to the Canterbury Tales
The Pardoner's Tale
The Wife of Bath's Prologue and Tale

Caryl Churchill
Top Girls

John Clare
Selected Poems

Joseph Conrad
Heart of Darkness

Charles Dickens
Bleak House
Great Expectations
Hard Times

Carol Ann Duffy
Selected Poems
The World's Wife

George Eliot
Middlemarch
The Mill on the Floss

T. S. Eliot
Selected Poems
The Waste Land

Sebastian Faulks
Birdsong

F. Scott Fitzgerald
The Great Gatsby

John Ford
'Tis Pity She's a Whore

John Fowles
The French Lieutenant's Woman

Michael Frayn
Spies

Charles Frazier
Cold Mountain

Brian Friel
Making History
Translations

William Golding
The Spire

Thomas Hardy
Jude the Obscure
The Mayor of Casterbridge
The Return of the Native
Selected Poems
Tess of the d'Urbervilles

Nathaniel Hawthorne
The Scarlet Letter

Seamus Heaney
Selected Poems from 'Opened Ground'

Homer
The Iliad
The Odyssey

Khaled Hosseini
The Kite Runner

Aldous Huxley
Brave New World

Henrik Ibsen
A Doll's House

James Joyce
Dubliners

John Keats
Selected Poems

Philip Larkin
High Windows
The Whitsun Weddings and Selected Poems

Ian McEwan
Atonement

Christopher Marlowe
Doctor Faustus
Edward II

Arthur Miller
All My Sons
Death of a Salesman

John Milton
Paradise Lost Books I and II

George Orwell
Nineteen Eighty-Four

Sylvia Plath
Selected Poems

William Shakespeare
Antony and Cleopatra
As You Like It
Hamlet
Henry IV Part I
King Lear
Macbeth
Measure for Measure
The Merchant of Venice
A Midsummer Night's Dream
Much Ado About Nothing
Othello
Richard II
Richard III
Romeo and Juliet
The Taming of the Shrew
The Tempest
Twelfth Night
The Winter's Tale

Mary Shelley
Frankenstein

Richard Brinsley Sheridan
The School for Scandal

Bram Stoker
Dracula

Alfred Tennyson
Selected Poems

Alice Walker
The Color Purple

John Webster
The Duchess of Malfi
The White Devil

Oscar Wilde
The Importance of Being Earnest
The Picture of Dorian Gray
A Woman of No Importance

Tennessee Williams
Cat on a Hot Tin Roof
The Glass Menagerie
A Streetcar Named Desire

Jeanette Winterson
Oranges Are Not the Only Fruit

Virginia Woolf
To the Lighthouse

William Wordsworth
The Prelude and Selected Poems

Wordsworth and Coleridge
Lyrical Ballads

Poetry of the First World War